# Consuming

# Consuming Passion

**Why the killing of Jesus really matters**

Edited by
SIMON BARROW AND
JONATHAN BARTLEY

DARTON · LONGMAN + TODD

First published in 2005 by
Darton, Longman and Todd Ltd
1 Spencer Court
140–142 Wandsworth High Street
London
SW18 4JJ

Reprinted 2007

ISBN 10: 0–232–52607–9
ISBN 13: 978–0–232–52607–3

A catalogue record for this book is available from the British
Library.




Phototypeset by Intype Libra Ltd, London
Printed and bound in Great Britain by
Intype Libra Ltd, London

# Contents

# Acknowledgements

The editors would like to thank all who have contributed essays to this book. The bulk of the material appears in this collection for the first time. Ched Myers' article is a considerably abbreviated version of 'The Passion: The Gospel as Political Parody', which first appeared in *The Witness* magazine in the USA ([http://thewitness.org/](http://thewitness.org/)) in April 2004. Giles Fraser's chapter is distilled from two articles in the *Guardian*, plus insights shared on BBC Radio 4's *Thought for the Day*, to which he is a regular contributor. We are also grateful to J. Denny Weaver for allowing us to edit material from his paper to the European Mennonite Theology Forum meeting in London last year. Lastly James Alison's thought-provoking reflections on the resurrection in relation to the Passion narratives are excerpted from his excellent book *The Joy of Being Wrong: Original Sin through Easter Eyes* (New York: Crossroad Herder, 1998).

# Introduction: Why talk about the cross really matters

## Simon Barrow and Jonathan Bartley

The arrival of a new theological title on the bookshelves is usually something of a non-event as far as the general media is concerned. 'Christians talking to themselves', is the usual verdict – and, what's even worse, Christians talking in a specialist vocabulary that not only makes no sense to non-initiates, but has few obvious points of plausible, useful contact with the world everyone else seems to live in. In short, it's completely irrelevant.

There's no guarantee that *Consuming Passion* won't be received with the same collective yawn, of course. But there are plenty of reasons for recognising that it's not that kind of book. For a start, its core topic, though framed around an event that animates specifically Christian worship, thought, practice and argument throughout the world (the killing of Jesus), is thereby about something that interests and affects everyone. Life and death. More than that, life *versus* death. In order to see why, let's start by getting our bearings. Then we will look at the specific contributions to this book, and how you might choose to find your way around them.

Christian talk that's thoughtful, substantial and useful (what gets called 'Christian theology' in the jargon)[1] isn't about the petty concerns of an isolated, self-referring tribe. Not if it's done properly. It's about the question of how we actually learn to make sense of the world, whether there is any hope for us all, where we are coming from, what life's about, where we are heading, and how we might get somewhere.

Of course 'the secular world' long ago gave up any serious thought that Christians, or people of any other

1

institutional religious tradition, had anything worthwhile to say about things that really matter. Recognising much God-talk to be circular, obscure, delusional and pointless, it decided (with Nietzsche) that 'God is dead' and that whatever language we use to unpack the possible meanings of life and death must be one we create, not one we inherit . . . and especially not one we inherit from 'religious people' (like those who conspired in killing Jesus, perhaps?).

So far, so understandable. But then a funny thing happened. Just as all the pundits and sociologists were talking about religion being on the way out, suddenly it became big again. Massive, in fact. And not always for good reasons. On the one hand, we have the strange phenomenon of 'rational people' who are supposedly secure in autonomous, self-legitimating scientific reason hanging out crystals and getting involved with a range of practices usually dubbed 'new age'. On the other hand, we see the resurgence of powerful religious movements that unite a supposedly 'traditional, fundamental' understanding of faith to substantial political power and deadly arsenals.

The persistence of the 'Christian Right' in the US, and the rise of radical Islamism in the Muslim world, along with narrow Hindu nationalism, Jewish rejectionism, armed Buddhism (yes, really) and angry Sikhism, scares the wits out of secularists. They often haven't got a clue what to do. Apart, that is, from shouting back, dismissing them all as mad, or striking political poses which often make the problem worse – because these are just as irrational and intolerant behaviour patterns as those they contend. Oddly enough these are the tactics that *both* President Bush (versus Islamism) *and* some of the liberal left (versus militantly conservative Christianity) end up using, though not with any degree of equivalence or intent.

One huge problem with all this is that, even if it had its analysis right, it just couldn't work. Bombing doesn't make enemies comply; it just makes them get their own bombs. Banning headscarves doesn't make Muslims tolerant, just fed up and resentful. Assuming that faith is an antonym to reason doesn't make religious conviction go away, it just stokes its anger. And yelling doesn't make a problem disappear, it just leaves you feeling a bit better about yourself while everything remains the same.

There has to be another way. This book seeks to show what it is. While by no means agreeing on everything, the contributors to this volume think that many Christians have seriously misconstrued the central components and narratives of Christian talk about the death of Jesus and how this offers hope and life to the world. And they say that this matters a great deal, whether you are a Christian or not, because theories of religious conviction that depend upon dividing the world into victim and victimiser – and then using the language, assumptions and tactics of the *victimiser* – are positively dangerous. They lead to suffering, torture and death, both physically and psychologically.

One contributor, the Baptist minister and social activist Steve Chalke, goes so far as to reiterate the accusation that the 'penal substitution' understanding of the atonement (Christian theory about how the death of Jesus changes the world) is tantamount to 'cosmic child abuse'. That's a pretty massive accusation. And if it is anywhere near correct, you can see that holding wrong-headed notions of Christian doctrine could end up subliminally reinforcing or legitimating behaviour that causes actual harm in the real world. No small issue.

So why not abandon this talk about Jesus and his death altogether? That's what most secularists ask. Or, at least, keep it to yourself and don't bother us. There are two reasons why this isn't on. First, as we see these days every time we open a newspaper, we no longer live in a world where it is possible (if it ever was) simply to put each other in boxes and throw away the key. The ideas and rituals of other people may be anathema to you, but they won't disappear or cease having their impact. And if those people get power, they might make life hell for you and others (and themselves).

Second, there are some very strong reasons for thinking that, in this case, if our talk about Jesus and his death can be *redeemed*, reclaimed from wrong-headedness, then we might actually be on to something that is not only wholesome but truly liberating. 'Saving', as Christians claim. The authors in this volume make this case too, and they begin to demonstrate that the specificity of Christian language and experience puts us in touch with something that purely secular thought cannot.

That 'something' is God as we never understood God before – the God who, far from being a 'tribal deity' or a theory about the world rendered impotent by metaphysics and scientific understanding, is actually the kind of patient, dependable, de-centring, non-violent, inviting, transforming and (very important, this) non-manipulative love made available to us in the life, death and resurrection of Jesus.

Now these are big claims and they aren't going to be resolved or 'proved' in one volume. But they are what the essays in *Consuming Passion* are about. What's more (and what will be just as shocking to some religionists and some secularists alike), these essays expose the wrong-headedness about some Christian theories of the cross not by dismissing the tradition, but by deploying it more thoroughly and justifiably. By being better traditionalists, that is.

This is a shock because most people, and certainly most people in the general media, have decided that there are two kinds of Christians. First, there are the 'conservatives': the 'evangelicals' and the 'fundamentalists'.[2] They believe in 'traditional' and 'orthodox' Christian claims. Then there are 'liberals' and 'modernisers' who want to 're-write', 'abandon' or 'replace' the traditional and the orthodox with something else. Even Christians seem to believe this is true, and helpfully organise themselves into warring camps along just these kind of lines.[3]

The problem is, this is a hopelessly simplistic and misleading picture – not because it doesn't have any element of veracity, but because mostly it misrepresents what is really at stake in theological argument. The writers in this volume are all mainstream Christian believers who show that these caricatures fail. They believe strongly in the central categories of historic, biblical Christian faith. But they think that these work quite differently to the way they function in the 'what everybody knows is the case' thinking of dogmatists on all sides. So they defy easy labels.

What the different writers argue – in different ways, with different emphases, and with different outcomes – is that

4

what is *thought* to be 'orthodox' or 'traditional' Christian thought is often nothing of the sort. It can sometimes be a hotchpotch of half-understood doctrine read back into a patchwork of mostly misunderstood biblical texts, all filtered through Christian communities which should (but usually don't) think about these things very much.

The result is that some rather short-sighted people with a lot of power and influence are able to colonise Christian faith and language for malign purposes like justifying social injustice, buttressing their own sanctity at the expense of others, and controlling the 'Christian economy' of thought and life with angry denunciations or expulsions of anyone who dares to question their monopoly.[4] Some would say that this is what has happened to Steve Chalke in the hands of some (but by no means all) members of the Evangelical Alliance in the UK. It is not without significance that when he and Alan Mann wrote their little book *The Lost Message of Jesus* (Zondervan, 2004), a few people murmured, perhaps without much thought about what they were really saying, 'he'll get crucified for this.'[5]

Which brings us back to the cross and its meaning. *Consuming Passion* has a certain logic to its running order, and there are a number of ways you might choose to read it – depending on your degree of prior understanding, your interests, and whether you are approaching it as a believing Christian, an enquirer, a member of another faith community, or a well-rehearsed sceptic.

Though the idea that thinking hard about religion is unnecessary and impossible is now very common currency, inconveniently for those who would prefer to avoid it, it isn't true. So no matter how good a theologian might be, she or he *will* have to use some specialist language and refer to conversations (or images) from the past which aren't *immediately* going to grab everyone's attention or sort it all out for them. That is certainly the case in the area of 'atonement' theory and Christian understandings of the significance of Jesus' death. But there is a point to it.

The point is that what is discussed here isn't something people have just started to dream up. It has been talked about for hundreds (nay, thousands) of years, and the idea that our forbears in faith and reason were simple, stupid or

5

deluded people from whom we have nothing to learn, and with whom no cultural contact is possible, is a peculiarly (post)modern conceit that impoverishes us all. If you aren't prepared to entertain that possibility, then we respectfully suggest that you go away now and only talk to people who already agree with your own existing biases and mores.

For everyone else (see, you *are* still there!), our suggestions are as follows. If you are approaching this topic very much from 'the outside', you might find it helpful to start with Giles Fraser's essay, because it has been adapted from material he first wrote for the *Guardian* and broadcast on the BBC. This doesn't *guarantee* that the average suburban atheist (or *Daily Telegraph* reader!) is going to agree with all of it, or instantly care about Christian doctrine. But it does explain why what it deals with is a matter of life and death for everyone, not just the religious.

Fraser is a believer who operates thoughtfully on the territory non-believers feel more comfortable with. Steve Chalke, on the other hand, gives a picture to us of what it is like to see things (and to change your mind) from deep *within* a traditional, faithful, biblical Christian framework – discovering God's gift in Jesus again, as for the first time. His is an intra-Christian argument. He summarises from a radical evangelical angle what the cross is all about.

Then Stuart Murray, another creative evangelical theologian, this time in the Anabaptist tradition, begins to delve into history and to explain why and how things got messed up by the onset of 'Christendom' (the alliance of religion with imperial power, and all that has flowed from this). Historically, Anabaptists were killed by the self-appointed orthodox for daring to point out that their interpretations were perhaps not as orthodox as (and much more harmful than) they had figured; so this isn't a polite, arcane little argument, you understand.[5]

Vic Thiessen, a Mennonite, then raises for the first time a significant ghost at this feast, albeit one about to be made very real. This is film-maker Mel Gibson and his movie *The Passion of the Christ*. He gently introduces the idea that Gibson's account of the Passion narratives may be neither very accurate (in terms of the actual content and emphases of the different gospel writers' accounts), nor especially good for our religious health.

Thiessen then gives an airing to the different 'major families of thought' about the cross and its meaning. Chalke and Murray have already referred to these, and they will recur several times again in this collection, in different degrees of detail. This isn't unnecessary repetition that the editors couldn't be bothered to excise. It's a reflection of the fact that these foundational ideas need to be unpacked and re-packed again and again, from a number of distinct angles, if we are going to get hold of their importance and argue with them properly.

Those unfamiliar with historical Christian theology – which unfortunately is likely to include a lot of faithful Christians, these days – should be warned that some of the ideas and arguments Thiessen rehearses here might at first seem rather arcane and off-the-wall. This is because we are not accustomed to the same way of looking at the world as many of our forbears. But their thought still works away in our culture, and often pops up in unexpected places: for instance to influence or block our reading of biblical texts without us even realising it. This happens a lot in both evangelical and secular circles, where 'what the Bible says' often turns out to be 'what people we know have told us it says' (to the extent that we now find it hard to see that it actually *doesn't*).

Next, there is a substantial contribution from another Mennonite scholar, J. Denny Weaver. He seeks to generate an alternative (but tradition-faithful) re-working of one of the historic 'doctrines' of the cross, based upon and reinforcing a view of non-violence as an essential component of the core of the Christian message, not some arguable bolt-on for a few who like that sort of thing. It is by following Jesus in his refusal of violence that Christian faith becomes both redeeming and redeemed in a violent, unjust world, argues Weaver (in agreement with most of the other contributors here).

Meanwhile, heavyweight US activist-theologian Ched Myers non-violently demolishes Mel Gibson's film with a compelling, detailed reading of St Mark's Passion story, to show that the God who is involved with the cruel, political and horrific execution of Jesus is not a God who enjoys, inflicts or legitimates such suffering and oppression, but is, rather, the One who stands against it – even to the point of enduring it and transforming it into something pro-life and anti-death. We are on difficult, hilly ground here: 'deep territory'. But the air is bracing and enlivening.

Anne Richards,[6] however, takes us straight back into the clutches of hell, but imaginatively and redeemingly. A scholar of English who now works as a practical theologian, Richards was revolted when she first saw Gibson's *The Passion*. Then she realised that it is sick precisely because it really *is* set in hell. The film provokes the question, 'what does the world look like as a hellish nightmare, what does it look like in our current estimation, and what might it look like if it was actually God's good creation?' (our paraphrase). Richards challenges us to ask which of these accounts of the world is right, how we will know, and how we will live differently depending on our answer.

As something of a counterpoint, Kevin Scully, an Anglican Catholic priest and writer in the east end of London, looks at how the religious (and not-so-religious) imagination of the crucifixion and the way of the cross really works in our street iconography, our churches and our communities. He draws some surprising conclusions about how Christian people might become something other than 'the church of the bloody useless' – in the process of dealing with real blood and real uselessness (as God does in Christ), and not separating themselves from participation in such things.

Next, theologian Michael Northcott revisits the problems of (allegedly 'faithful') dominant Christian understandings of what it means to say that 'Christ has died for our sins', with specific reference to their use by the American Religious Right and its new imperial project. He also revisits his own youth, and figures out why he was able to dissent from the dominant Christian mindset at his university in order to rediscover a different biblical pattern of believing, belonging and behaving.

Simon Barrow, an ecumenist and theologian, follows this up with an article that shows just how extraordinarily *offensive* everyday Christian speech and imagery about the crucifixion is. It ought to be offensive, he says, because it is God's shocking, real satire of the death-dealing ways we are immersed in as both secular and religious people. To preach 'Christ crucified' is an absolute scandal, but it is a scandal with a point and a possibility of hope that is otherwise entirely missing from the political satire of which it is the most breathtaking form. Chris Morris and *Jerry Springer: The Opera* 'eat your heart out', says Barrow. Christians who attack the 'blasphemy' of such things are missing the whole point of the Gospel, which is that the salvation God offers is mortgaged on what, in human estimation, is the *ultimate* proof that 'nothing is sacred'. A demeaning death. What we discover when we are baptised into the death and risen life of Jesus, however, is that *everything* can be sacred, but only if God is who God is in Christ, reconciling the world.

Hope is where this collection rests. Not an easy or facile hope, but one which struggles with death in order to discover a life that does not efface, deny, inflict or ignore it – but rather endures, absorbs and transforms it. This is the eternal life of God, displayed in and as Jesus through the disturbance of the Spirit. First David Wood, an Australian priest, begins with the world of art and the senses to explore how it is, in the mysterious economy of God generated by the Gospel, that light becomes visible in (rather than out of) the shadows and the dark. The 'luminous darkness' of the cross is nothing like expectable, and is therefore only available as pure gift. But it is exactly because it stands beyond our propensity for control and domination that it brings us to life again, and delivers us from false religion. Nothing else can do this. As Barrow argues earlier, 'the (true) atheism of the cross is sufficient in a way that simply trying not to believe in the powers-that-be in our own strength never can be.'

To finish, we have a profound meditation from leading Catholic theologian James Alison, someone lauded by, among others, the current Archbishop of Canterbury, Dr Rowan Williams. Alison explores and explains the meaning of the resurrection of Jesus (which turns out to be as far from a clichéd 'escape to victory' as it is possible to get) and what he calls 'the intelligence of the victim'.

We cannot and should not try to get away from the fact that what stands at the heart of the Christian message *is* a victim. Nietzsche recognised this in a way that many believers have not, but he drew exactly the wrong estimations of Jesus, God, the world, humanity and himself from his realisation.[7] This is because he too remained mired in that victimology and corresponding power-quest that enslaves all human beings, but he decided that the way forward was to abandon the one thing that can address it. The anti-sacrificial death of Jesus. James Alison, who has drawn deeply on the work of cultural anthropologist and literary critic René Girard, begins to show how and why the Gospel of Christ's death and risen life is substantial good news. But only if it is taken out of the hands of death-dealers.[8]

In conclusion, this book is (we hope) exciting, change-making, creatively traditional, life-affirming Christian thinking for people who thought such a thing was impossible – both on the pews, and beyond them. It certainly doesn't claim all the answers, but it is a step on the journey towards a consuming Passion that remakes us rather than breaks us. Which is what the world needs above all else right now. And always.

## Notes

1 There are, of course, 'theologies' in the other major world religions. And they deserve to be taken seriously. But we write as Christians, convinced that what is said in the Christian community *is* a matter of life-or-death, and recognising that being competent at speaking one language doesn't automatically qualify you to use or speak another. So the fact that we are writing about Christian theology should not be taken to mean that we regard other religious thought systems as secondary or unimportant. Since Jesus famously used a Samaritan (a heretic on the edge of his own religious world) as an exemplar of faith-in-action, Christians have no excuse for writing off 'the religious other'. We just feel that it's better to engage on the basis of getting our own house in order, rather than sallying into others' territory with insufficient regard for the differences of custom and understanding. We hope that will be recognised by those Christians deeply engaged in inter-faith conversation (which includes a number who have contributed to this book), as well as those who think such engagement is dangerous or unnecessary.

2 Actually these descriptors are far from synonyms for one group of people, but in a religiously illiterate age they are often used in that way.

3 Many of the contributors to this book, who span a wide range of church traditions and 'theologies', write for – or are linked by – Ekklesia, the UK Christian think tank. See www.ekklesia.co.uk. Part of Ekklesia's job is to defy categories. It has been described by the *Daily Telegraph* as 'liberal' and by the *Church Times* as 'evangelical'. Neither is adequate. We need to think harder and better. 'Anabaptist-influenced' would be true, however.

4 The fantastic irony of all this, of course, is that this is exactly the kind of thing that Jesus was up against in the religious and political culture of his time. Indeed, it is part of the reason he ended up getting killed.

5 'Anabaptist' was originally a term of abuse used by other Christians against small, pietistic sects during the Reformation. It means 're-baptiser'. The Anabaptists were people who wanted to get back to New Testament Christianity in the face of what they saw as the corruption of state churches. They did not regard automatic, compulsory 'christening' as legitimate baptism, which meant being received into a believers' community. Though some Anabaptists became what we would see as sectarian crazies, many were peace-loving and peace-making followers of Jesus who thought that faith needed to show itself in good behaviour, as a witness to the world. Among their descendants today are the Mennonites. In the UK, see: http://www.anabaptistnetwork.com/.

6 Richards is one of only two women who have contributed to this volume. There are also no black people or people from outside the Western world. It was extremely unfortunate that the timing of this project meant that a significant number of women and black people we approached were unable to contribute. We do not shy from criticism on this point. But the contributors have sought to take their own limitations (and the powerful perspectives of those who *do* represent such wider interests) very seriously. We acknowledge that this is a book of 'Western theology', but we would argue that there is nothing wrong with Westerners taking 'their own stuff' seriously and not patronising others with tokenism. Similarly, some writers use male pronouns for the divine, without supposing them to render God male, while others seek to avoid this. We have left things as they are, but the editors are committed to inclusive language, and learning from our problems with language.

7 See, however, Giles Fraser, *Redeeming Nietzsche: The piety of unbelief* (Routledge, 2003).

8 James Alison, like many of the writers represented in this book, has written extensively and in great detail about these issues. No one is pretending that what is within these covers is adequate to present, explain and defend all the arguments offered in this introduction. But they give a good starting point.

# 1 The Easter of hawks, doves, victims and victimisers

**Giles Fraser**

The Passion offers Christians no comfortable space from which to be on the side of the victim. During the liturgy of Holy Week, people who shout 'Hosanna' on Palm Sunday are the same people who shout 'Crucify' on Good Friday. The fact that the crucifixion has been the basis for centuries of anti-Semitic propaganda must remind all Christians of their own capacity for violence and brutality. The dangers of imagining oneself a weeping onlooker again leaves a fundamental complacency fully intact.[1]

A meditation upon the shamefulness of Christian history allows Christians their most valuable insight: that there is no safe or comfortable perspective from which to stand aloof from any complicity with the horrors of the world. In my darker moments I am ashamed to be a Christian. As a Jewish Christian, I often fear that in converting to Christianity I sided with the persecutors against the persecuted. But this shame at complicity with a culture of oppression allows for a more general sensitivity to the ways we are all compromised by the endemic violence of the world. The desire to inhabit a cultural space that is unblemished is a dangerous fantasy that cooperates with the desire to avoid facing one's own capacity for brutality. Dr Jekyll's fundamental flaw is his refusal to acknowledge the existence of Mr Hyde. Hyde can only operate in the dark, in the unexamined spaces brought about by Jekyll's pious avoidance of his own darker motivations. For Jekyll and Hyde are not two people but one. Tenderness, intelligence and brutality easily co-exist in the same person. Our own cruelties and prejudices are given ideal conditions to grow when we refuse to admit to them. Let me give some examples

In 1990 the sociologist Gillian Rose became a consultant for the Polish Commission for the Future of Auschwitz. From then until her death in 1995, she argued that the Holocaust was being narrated in such a way as to protect the present generation from the thought that they too might have something in common with the perpetrators. For Rose, the story of the Holocaust is typically told so as to place the audience alongside the victim. The crisis of glimpsing our own reflection in the face of the Nazi camp guard is a horror too far.

Thus the closing scene of the film *Schindler's List* leaves us, in her words, 'piously joining the survivors putting stones on Schindler's grave in Israel'. Despite the experience of overwhelming repulsion at the horror of Nazi genocide, too often a fundamental complacency is left unexamined. 'Instead of emerging with sentimental tears, which leave us emotionally and politically intact,' Rose said, 'we [ought to] emerge with the dry eyes of a deep grief which belongs to the recognition of our ineluctable grounding in the norms of the emotional and political culture represented.'

Rose was a Jewish scholar who was baptised on her deathbed. I do not know whether she shared my feelings of guilt, but she was far from unknowing about what was at stake. Her attack upon those narratives that place us tearfully alongside the victim is an attack upon the refusal of the Jekyll in each of us to admit to the Hyde in all of us.

Christians often engage with the Holocaust by celebrating the courage of other Christians who resisted the Nazis: people like Dietrich Bonhoeffer, Martin Niemoller and Edith Stein. But the truth is, they were rare exceptions. For centuries, many Christians have stoked the fires of anti-Semitism with lies and slander. Jews were blamed for the death of Christ. Some believed that Jews practised child sacrifice. The fourth-century saint and theologian Gregory of Nyssa called the Jews 'companions of the devil, accursed, detested, enemies of all that is beautiful'.[2]

Martin Luther went even further: 'We are at fault in not slaying them,' he said. 'Rather we allow them to live freely

13

in our midst despite all their murdering, cursing, blaspheming, lying.' He went on to advise Christians to 'set fire to their synagogues and schools and to bury and cover with dirt whatever will not burn.' These days, Christians are ashamed by such words. But it's still terribly important to remember them and to understand where they came from; how the religion of the Crucified Lamb could become the religion that slaughtered lambs.[3]

My worry is that the identification with the victims when we remember the Holocaust protects many of us from the much more disturbing thought that we may have something in common with the perpetrators. Placing oneself alongside the victim may leave intact a fundamental complacency about our own potential for violence and hatred. The idea that we might catch a glimpse of our own reflection in the face of a Nazi guard is a terrifying thought – but one that is more likely to lead to genuine transformation than a cheap identification with the victim, which, too often, is more about telegraphing our own compassion for others to see.

Often, of course, we protect ourselves from the thought of our own capacity for wickedness by describing wickedness as something foreign and alien. That's the problem with our tendency always to use the Nazis as the default example of human evil. It encourages the thought that evil is done by people with funny accents and sinister uniforms, people who lived in the past, people very different from us. But as Eric Fromm once put it: 'As long as one believes that the evil man wears horns, one will not discover an evil man.'

The most terrifying message of European anti-Semitism is that evil is perpetrated by ordinary, apparently respectable men and women with nice families and good taste in wine and music. In other words: by people like you and me. Those who refuse to face it are often the most dangerous people of all.

I was once sent an Easter card from a group of Palestinian Christians, drawing attention to the fact that the anniversary of the Deir Yassin massacre fell that year on Good Friday. Before dawn on the morning of 9 April 1948, Jewish paramilitaries launched a surprise attack

upon the quiet Palestinian village of Deir Yassin just outside Jerusalem. Soldiers went from house to house shoot-
ing old men, women and children. A group of Palestinian
prisoners were paraded in trucks, taken to the local quarry,
lined up and then shot.

Fahimeh Ali Mustafa Zeidan, then aged eleven,
described what happened: 'They blew the door down,
entered and started searching the place; they got to the
store room, and took us out one by one. Then they called
my brother Mahmoud and shot him in our presence; and
when my mother screamed and bent over my brother, carrying my little sister Khadra, who was still being breast-
fed, they shot my mother too. Then they lined us up, shot
at us, and left.' For the Palestinians, the massacre at Deir
Yassin marks the symbolic beginning of their story of dis-
possession and exile.

The card goes on to make the point that 'Deir Yassin
stands, unnamed and unmarked, in clear sight of the
Holocaust memorial at Yad Vashem' – a reminder that the
massacre at Deir Yassin occurred within three years of the
liberation of Auschwitz. There is of course no equivalence
between Deir Yassin and the Holocaust. Furthermore, the
point of comparison is badly made precisely because it is
not disturbing enough. For Palestinian Christians to use
Good Friday as an opportunity to reflect upon the inter-
changeability of victim and perpetrator ought to remind
them of the Passion's exposure of our uneasy ambivalence
about identifying with victims and acting as victimisers.

Nor is this simply a meditation for the religious. For the
cultural space that often has little sense of its own complicity in the horrors of the world is that of secular modernity.
The new Jekyll and Hyde is the Jekyll of democratic liber-
alism and the Hyde of religious fanaticism. Newspaper
cartoons often show those with religious belief as crazed
and vicious. Good Friday is a day to admit that Christians
are often guilty as charged.

But does the attack upon religious fanaticism also work
in a dangerous way to excuse the secular imagination an
insight into its own capacity for violence? What secular
liturgies are there to reveal that those who shout 'Hosanna'
are the same people who shout 'Crucify'? For the

15

Holocaust may have taken place in a country shaped by the values of Christianity. But it took place in a country no less shaped by the values of the Enlightenment and modernity as well. Figures recently released by the Israeli Government reveal a marked rise in anti-Semitic attacks in Britain. Sixty years after the Holocaust, the greatest crime of the twentieth century, the curse of anti-Semitism continues to haunt us.

All this brings us back to the fact that there are two archetypal ways of understanding the theology of Easter: one is structured around the notion of retribution; the other around the notion of forgiveness. As theological literacy becomes increasingly necessary to decode what many of our world leaders are really saying, this distinction is crucial. Easter has its hawks and its doves, as well as its victimisers and victims.[4]

The Easter of the hawks insists that sin always has to be balanced, or paid for, with pain. It's the theological equivalent of the refusal to be 'soft on crime'. From this perspective, as we will observe in different ways throughout this book, Easter is the story of Jesus paying off the debt of human sin with his own suffering and death. As the popular Easter hymn 'There is a Green Hill Far Away' puts it: 'There was no other good enough to pay the price of sin.' Retribution is a moral necessity because through it the scales of justice are righted. Sin must be paid for with blood, just as crime must be paid for by punishment. On the cross Jesus is taking the punishment that is properly ours.

What is remarkable about this theology of debt is that it is precisely what Jesus rejects when he invokes the spirit of the Jubilee at the outset of his ministry. The Jubilee tradition argues for the regular unilateral remission of debt so that people are not imprisoned by a liability they cannot ever meet. It's a tradition that has been powerfully invoked in relation to third-world debt, though many have little grasp of its biblical provenance. This is Jesus' good news to the poor and freedom to the captive. For the hawks, however, the spirit of the Jubilee is a theological free lunch.

But the problem with the Easter of the hawks is much more than theological. The idea that human salvation is premised upon the torture and murder of an innocent life is one that has systematically weakened the capacity of European culture to set itself against cruelty. The glorification of pain and blood as the route to salvation has gone hand in hand with an obnoxious aesthetic of sadism. The 'Christian' idea that pain and guilt must be in cosmic balance has led generations of Christians to support the death penalty, leave the criminal justice system unchallenged and oppose prison reform.

It is no coincidence that places where this sort of theology has flourished – in seventeenth-century England and twenty-first-century America – are places where justice has been, and continues to be, expressed through the scaffold or the electric chair. From his house in South Molton Street, William Blake could see processions of the condemned making their way up Oxford Street to the gallows at Tyburn. In what Blake took to be the ultimate betrayal of Christ, the church justified this slaughter by appealing to Christ's sufferings on the cross. Blake was characteristically fierce in his denunciation: 'Every religion that preaches vengeance for sin is the religion of the enemy and avenger and not the forgiver of sin and their God is Satan.'

Like many others before and since, Blake drew upon an alternative reading of Easter. Here the defining feature of Christ's moral teaching is an opposition to the retributive ethic encapsulated in many interpretations of the principle of an eye for an eye and a tooth for a tooth.[5] Rather, Christ offered an ethic based upon forgiveness – on a refusal to become a mirror image to the violent other. In doing this he threatened to put a great deal of established religion out of business. For this established religion, based as it was on the practice of cultic sacrifice, was a way for the community to launder its own proclivity for violent reciprocity. Religion provided a safe redirection of the violent impulse and its temporary catharsis in the bloody sacrifice of small animals.

Jesus, however, takes up an alternative tradition found in the psalms and the writings of the prophets: 'I desire mercy and not sacrifice,' Jesus repeats from the book of Hosea. He thus attacks the religious authorities and is murdered for so doing. Jesus does not oppose the brutality of

17

his treatment by an equal and opposite show of force. And in not returning violence with violence he initiates a fragile and vulnerable community of non-retaliation known as the kingdom of God. 'No future without forgiveness' is how Archbishop Desmond Tutu summed up the theology that decisively shaped the Truth and Reconciliation Commission as it sought to deal with Apartheid. The same spirit is just as necessary in taking forward the aptly named Good Friday agreement.

Despite this alternative tradition, the punitive voice of Christianity continues to exert considerable influence on public policy, not least in the US. Here a retributive doctrine of the cross is the key link between fundamentalist Christianity and right-wing politics. It's a cultural context that makes possible the question of whether torture is a legitimate means of interrogating terrorists. It's a context that encourages the belief that the tragedy of 9/11 has to be paid for with the blood of another. It's not blood for oil, as the posters say. Worse than that – it's blood for blood. This is the theology that underpins the moral convictions of the White House. And it's one Christ died opposing.

## Notes

1 The opening part of this article is adapted from the author's 'The dry eyes of deep grief', *Guardian*, Friday 9 April 2004, the anniversary of the execution of Christian theologian Dietrich Bonhoeffer at Flossenberg, a Nazi concentration camp, in 1944.

2 The reflection on the Holocaust was first given by Giles Fraser as part of a BBC Radio 4 'Thought for the Day' in February 2005.

3 The latter phrase is adapted from Simon Barrow, writing on www.ekklesia.co.uk.

4 From the author's 'Easter's hawks and doves', *Guardian*, Friday 18 April 2003.

5 The idea of the *Lex Talionis* can in fact be seen as a limit on violence preventing escalations in tit-for-tat retaliation. Another way of interpreting it is: 'An eye for an eye . . . but no more.'

# 2 Redeeming the cross from death to life

## Steve Chalke

'He was wounded for our transgressions . . . by his stripes we are healed' (Isaiah 53:5). Powerful words. But what exactly do they mean? And what are the implications of this statement today for us as individuals, for the church as a whole and for wider society? The answer Christians give to the simple, yet profound, question about the meaning of the atonement is all important because, as we shall see, inadequate doctrines of atonement lead to inadequate doctrines of God, humanity and mission.

What we believe shapes the way that we behave. Behaviour is always linked to belief. What we believe about the cross (and what God was doing there) will therefore fundamentally shape our attitude to, and involvement with, wider society. The way that people think of us is far more of an accurate reflection of who we are than we care to acknowledge. So if erroneous theology leads to dysfunctional missiology, could it be that there is there some connection between the public's almost universal perception of certain elements of the church as judgemental, guilt-inducing, censorious, finger-wagging, bigoted and self-righteous, and what we have come to believe about the cross?

Noted church historian David Bebbington claims that one of the four distinguishing features of evangelicalism is 'crucicentrism' (cross-centredness). But why is it that our culture now views the death of Christ as no more than some kind of ancient myth or irrelevant religious event? Perhaps one contributory factor is that our thinking about the cross has become distorted and thus our presentation of

it inadequate to engage the hearts and minds of our contemporaries.

Do Christians believe that Christ's death on the cross has
any relevance or significance beyond the individual eternal
destiny of his followers? What does the atonement mean
for the wider affairs of our communities; our government's
foreign policy; the war on terrorism; trade justice; people-
trafficking; the hopes, ambitions and fears of countless millions of people? What direction can our understanding of
the atonement offer as we think about the global challenges
faced by humanity at the beginning of the twenty-first century? Undoubtedly, a weakness of some modern atonement theology has been that it has simply failed to speak
to, engage with or challenge our culture in any significant
way.

If we are to take the New Testament seriously, we must
first acknowledge that any robust theology of the atonement is multicoloured rather than monochrome. No single
theory can ever capture its breadth and profundity. The
spectrum of complementary metaphors used by the writers
of the New Testament, in their attempt to express the truth
of the atonement, includes a clear substitutionary element
('The son of man came . . . to give his life as a ransom for
many') along with numerous others, among them
identification ('I want to know Christ and . . . the fellowship of his sufferings'), example ('Take up your cross and
follow me') and representation ('Through the disobedience
of one man many were made sinners, so through the obedience of one man the many will be made righteous').

However, what has become known as 'penal substitution' – the view of the cross which is an extremely commonly held model of atonement theory amongst many
evangelicals (penal referring to punishment, substitution
to Christ acting in our place) – does not fit comfortably
amongst these. The shadow it casts fails to match the picture of the cross painted by any of the New Testament
metaphors. Although in some circles it has been held to be
of huge importance, in my view it is simply not evident in
the biblical texts that are so often cited in its support.

Initially based upon (though not contained within) the
writings of Anselm of Canterbury (1033–1109), penal sub-

stitution was substantially formed by John Calvin's legal mind during the Reformation. As it is understood and taught today, primarily within evangelical circles, it rests largely on the work of the nineteenth-century American scholar Charles Hodge. A righteous God is angry with sinners and demands justice, he said. God's wrath can only be appeased through bringing about the violent death of his Son.

Many supporters of penal substitution, following Hodge's lead, tend to hold it as a 'God-given truth' – the only valid explanation of the atonement. Indeed, to question its legitimacy is viewed as tantamount to attacking the fundamentals of the faith itself. So it was that I recently had a conversation with one church leader who began by informing me that his view of the cross was '*the* biblical one'. For him penal substitution not only summed up everything there was to say about the significance of Christ's death, but acceptance of it was a non-negotiable baseline of authentic Christian faith.

However, the supposed orthodoxy of penal substitution is greatly overestimated, misleading even. Although it isn't as old as many people assume (it's not even as old as the pews in many of our church buildings), it is actually built on pre-Christian thought. This is a point pressed home by US scholar George Eldon Ladd in *A Theology of the New Testament*. He writes: 'In pagan Greek thought the gods often became angry with men, but their anger could be placated and the good will of the gods obtained by some kind of propitiatory sacrifice. Even in the Old Testament, the idea of atonement as the propitiating of an angry deity and transmuting his anger into benevolence is not to be found.'[1]

What we say about the atonement naturally flows out of our understanding of the character of God. I believe that the most profound theological truth expressed in the whole canon of Scripture is that 'God is love' (1 John 4:8). As Derek Tidball, principal of the London School of Theology, explains in *The Message of the Cross*: 'Love is not a quality that God possesses, but the essence of God himself. It is not a minor attribute that characterises God on occasions, but the very heart of God, his essential being. It is not a

21

component part of God, but his very nature. Before God is anything else, he is love.'[2]

So what of God's anger? It is an aspect of his love. Every father will be wronged by his children; it's a simple fact. All of us who know the joy of having children also know the pain of their rebelliousness – and yet no parent who loves their child ever seeks retribution for wrongs done to them. Anger that is motivated by genuine love cannot be violent or destructive.

The theological problem with penal substitution is that it presents us with a God who is first and foremost concerned with retribution flowing from wrath against sinners. The only way for God's anger to be placated is in receiving recompense from those who have wronged him; and although God's great love motivates him to send his Son, his wrath remains the driving force behind the need for the cross.

Of course, many Christians learn to live with this dichotomy. On the one hand they believe in God's grace and goodness, but on the other that one of the central acts of their faith is bound up in God's vengeance and wrath. The only way that they cope with this tension is simply to dismiss it as 'a divine paradox'. However, for the rest of the world, it is just a massive contradiction.

In *The Lost Message of Jesus*[3] I made the claim that penal substitution is tantamount to 'child abuse – a vengeful Father punishing his Son for an offence he has not even committed'. Though the sheer bluntness of this imagery (not original to me) shocked some, in reality it represents nothing more than a stark 'unmasking' of the violent, pre-Christian thinking behind such a theology. The simple truth is that if God does not relate to his only Son as a perfect father, neither can we relate to him as such.

If we follow Hodge's understanding of the atonement, then it is Jesus' death, no more and no less, that becomes our Gospel ('good news'). This reductionist approach downgrades the whole Gospel to a single sentence: 'God is no longer angry with us because Jesus died in our place.' Indeed, that is exactly why evangelistic presentations based on penal substitution often don't even bother to mention the resurrection because, for them, it serves no direct purpose in the story of our salvation.

Ironically, what Hodge most neglected was to let Jesus speak for himself. It is difficult to see how penal substitution fits with the words or attitude of Jesus. For instance, if the whole Gospel centres on Jesus' death, what was the good news he told his followers to preach (Luke 9:6) before the crucifixion? And if God needed a sacrifice to placate his anger, how could Jesus forgive sins before his sacrifice had been made? In fact, why did Jesus preach at all? The rest of his ministry was ultimately unnecessary if it is only his death that makes things new. Surely we can't embrace a theology in which Jesus' entire thirty-three-year incarnation could be reduced to a long weekend's activity.

It is interesting to note that in Jesus' own parabolic explanation of his Father's relationship with humankind, the prodigal son, the father is not presented as angry or vengeful or as seeking justice and retribution – instead he simply runs to greet his wayward child, showers him with gifts and welcomes him home. The father in the parable is wronged, but chooses to forgive in order to restore a broken relationship – there is no theme of retribution. Instead, the story is one of outstanding grace, of scandalous love and mercy – how different it would read if penal substitution was the model of atonement offered.

Then we come to Jesus' teachings on anger (Matthew 5:22) and retaliation (Matthew 5:38ff). Is it not strange for Jesus (God incarnate) on the one hand to teach 'do not return evil for evil' while still looking for retribution himself? Similarly wouldn't it be inconsistent for God to warn us not to be angry with each other and yet burn with wrath himself, or tell us to 'love our enemies' when he obviously couldn't quite bring himself to do the same without demanding massive appeasement? If these things are true, what does it mean to 'be perfect . . . as your heavenly Father is perfect' (Matthew 5:48)? If it is true that Jesus is 'the Word of God' then how can his message be inconsistent with his nature? If the cross has anything to do with penal substitution then Jesus' teaching becomes a divine case of 'do as I say, not as I do'. I, for one, believe that God practises what he preaches!

The charge that 'religion breeds violence' is one of the most common and popular complaints of all. But Jesus' message was unambiguous. Reciprocal violence is a vicious circle – a downward spiral. Vengeance always leads to reprisal. Hatred and suspicion breed hatred and suspicion. Once installed within a community they become self-perpetuating. Penal substitution theory betrays Jesus' attempt to root out the tendency of religion to lead to violence by inventing a theology of his death that is in direct opposition to his teaching. I am convinced that if the church could rediscover a deeper understanding of the cross we could once again speak with prophetic power to a society caught in the grip of the myth that violence can be redemptive.

The church's inability to shake off the great distortion of God contained in the theory of penal substitution, with its inbuilt belief in retribution and the redemptive power of violence, has cost us dearly. As the world struggles to find a way out of the chaos which is the consequence of the doctrine of 'might is right – he who has the biggest guns wins,' now is a moment for the church to live out its commitment to the ethic of non-violence lived out by Christ and ultimately demonstrated in his cross and resurrection.

But a commitment to penal substitution also raises wider ethical concerns. Indeed, it is open to the charge that it does little more than reflect the nineteenth- and twentieth-century culturally dominant values of individualism, autonomy, consumerism and empire. Therefore the primary purpose for the cross from humanity's point of view becomes its instant 'cash value'. By 'praying the prayer' I am immediately moved from the wrong side of God's legal ledger to the right side. The great transaction is done. And, what is more, not only am I no longer guilty, but I can also cling to the belief that 'once saved always saved'.

Penal substitution offers instant forgiveness without challenging basic day-to-day moral behaviour. It separates salvation from discipleship by disconnecting the way that Jesus lived his life from his saving work. More than that, it is also the case that because penal substitutionary theory tends to nurture a simplistic understanding of sin which is primarily individualistic and personal, it almost inevitably fails to address the corporate, systemic and endemic contexts of evil in our world. So it is no surprise that those who subscribe to this theory tend not be on the forefront of thinking about the major socio-political issues confronting us: about racial reconciliation, about issues of wealth and poverty, and about the environment.

But if penal substitution does not do justice to the story of our salvation through Christ, what other options are open to us? For me, the most empowering and motivating understanding of the atonement is that which, I believe, most closely resembles the thinking of the early church. As they struggled to make sense of Jesus' death and resurrection, the early church leaders (notably Irenaeus, Gregory of Nyssa and Origen) wrote about the cross in terms of a ransom. Of course, Jesus said himself that he came 'to give his life as a ransom for many' (Mark 10:45). But to whom was this ransom paid? The early church was adamant that it was not to God. As Origen put it: 'To whom did he give his life as a ransom for many? Assuredly not to God, could it then be to the Evil One? For he was holding fast until the ransom should be given him, even the life of Jesus; being deceived with the idea that he could have dominion over it, and not seeing that he could not bear the torture in retaining it.'[4]

From this commonly shared point of understanding a diversity of thinking slowly developed which sought to be faithful to the various pictures of the impact of the cross used by the different New Testament writers. Only in 1930 did Gustav Aulén coin the term *Christus Victor* (Christ the Conqueror), as a kind of 'umbrella' under which this spread of traditional understandings of the atonement could be gathered together. Within this, Christ's life, death *and* resurrection put together are seen as his victory over all the forces of evil and sin, including the earthly and spiritual powers that oppress people.

Indeed, it is Jesus' resurrection that gives the hope of the new heaven and the new earth, where sin is banished and all things are made right again. Jesus' emergence from the grave demonstrates that no political power, no unjust regime, no sinful structure can triumph, even in the infliction of death. It is Easter Sunday, not Good Friday, that shows the new kingdom in all its glory and God's love in all its fullness. On the cross Jesus does not placate God's anger in taking the punishment for sin, but rather absorbs its consequences and, as three days later he is raised, defeats death. It is the resurrection which finally puts the *Victor* in *Christus Victor*!

So it is that in and through Jesus' life, death and resurrection, God confronts and dethrones the powers of evil. But, in doing so, he will not use the tools of evil itself – those of coercion, unjust force, domination and violence. Instead, in 'weakness' he confounds satan. He lures wielders of unjust power into exposing and discrediting themselves. Jesus, creatively and courageously, armed only with the non-violent power of truth and love, opposes and defeats sin and violence. Jesus contains evil, but evil cannot contain him. Jesus soaks up all that satan can throw at him, but will not submit. The second Adam is tempted in a garden but will not succumb. Straining with every last effort and breath, he hangs on to his Father. Satan is overcome. Sin, evil and death itself are defeated.

As the New Testament makes abundantly clear the cross is cosmic, not just individual or personal, in its impact. Through Christ's life, death and resurrection, God – because of his great love for us – has intervened to repair his broken relationship with a world out of harmony with his purpose. Or, to conclude with the words of Gregory of Nyssa, 'Thus, life being introduced to the house of death, and light shining in darkness, that which is diametrically opposed to light and life might vanish; for it is not in the nature of darkness to remain when light is present, or of death to exist when life is active.'[5]

## Notes

1 George Eldon Ladd, *A Theology of the New Testament* (Eerdmans, 1974).
2 Derek Tidball, *The Message of the Cross* (IVP, 2001).
3 Steve Chalke, *The Lost Message of Jesus* (Zondervan, 2004).
4 Cf., Origen, *De Principiis*.
5 Gregory of Nyssa, *Catechetical Oration*, 5–32 (http://www.ccel.org/).

# 3 Rethinking atonement after Christendom

## Stuart Murray

Those who challenge established doctrinal or ethical perspectives frequently face two charges: that they are overturning traditional beliefs held by Christians throughout the centuries; and that, unduly influenced by contemporary culture, they are diluting or distorting their convictions for fear of offending current opinion.

Both charges have been levelled against those who have recently dared to challenge the penal substitution model of the atonement. For some evangelical Christians, penal substitution[1] is foundational to their understanding of salvation and close to the heart of their evangelical identity. Any critique of this interpretation of the atonement is so threatening that many are tempted to avoid engaging with the arguments by accusing critics of cultural compromise or disrespect for tradition.

Cultural compromise is an ever-present danger, as Christians throughout history have struggled to contextualise the Gospel authentically – remaining faithful to the Gospel story while retelling this story in fresh ways.[2] Indeed, 'traditional beliefs' often owe more to the cultural context within which they took shape than their defenders realise. Cultural changes may expose the influence of a fading culture and stimulate a healthy review of doctrinal and ethical convictions – a review that, rather than representing compromise with contemporary culture, liberates these convictions from inculturation in an earlier culture. Such a review may also reveal that supposedly traditional beliefs are, in fact, of relatively recent origin.

Penal substitution as an interpretation of the atonement emerged in the Reformation and post-Reformation era, although its classic definition was formulated only in the nineteenth century.[3] Many evangelicals, while recognising the validity of other models, have embraced this as their fundamental interpretation of the atonement. For most, what matters is its congruence with their understanding of key biblical texts,[4] rather than church tradition, though some have sought support for this model in the writings of various patristic theologians.[5] The popularity of penal substitution in contemporary evangelicalism has accorded this model an authority unwarranted by its quite recent articulation.

But not all evangelicals, let alone all Christians, have embraced penal substitution as the primary interpretation of the atonement. As a number of contributors to this book remind us, trenchant criticisms from black, feminist and womanist Christians have raised concerns about the capacity of this interpretation to offer good news to victims, the poor and the marginalised or to challenge injustice and institutional violence.[6] Growing numbers of evangelicals have also questioned the dominance of penal substitution, and some have suggested it is an illegitimate model of atonement. Reflection on the key biblical texts and the theological consequences of this model, engagement with contemporary culture and the history of the doctrine, as well as concern about the missiological and ethical implications of penal substitution, have led several evangelical scholars and leaders to dissent from this interpretation.[7]

Recent debates have indicated that such dissent is not limited to scholars but is much more widespread among evangelical Christians than was previously apparent. Steve Chalke's *The Lost Message of Jesus*,[8] the atonement content of which is summarised by a new essay here,[9] only repeats at a popular level what evangelical scholars have written on many occasions; but this has encouraged many members of evangelical churches openly to dissent from a belief they had struggled with but felt unable to challenge. The wrath this book has provoked – and the inevitable charges of cultural compromise and theological vandalism – indicates the level of threat felt by the guardians of an interpretation that is now under suspicion as a vestige of a fading culture rather than a vital foundation of (evangelical) Christianity.

This fading culture is the Christendom system and mindset that has dominated Europe since the fourth century and has been exported by mission and conquest to other parts of the world. Christendom has been gradually unravelling since at least the nineteenth century and the term 'post-Christendom' is increasingly used to describe the transitional era we are currently experiencing.[10] Whatever the achievements of Christendom, whether we regard it as a necessary phase or a disastrous compromise, whether we grieve or celebrate its demise, we must grapple with its legacy and try to discern what to carry with us into post-Christendom and what to leave behind.

Penal substitution is one aspect of this legacy – either an early consequence of the 'Christendom shift' if we trace its origins to the first great Christendom theologian, Augustine, or a vestige of the final centuries of Christendom if we accept its post-Reformation pedigree. Is this interpretation of atonement so immured in the fading culture of an oppressive sacral society that we should now abandon it and tell the story of Jesus after Christendom in fresh ways (or maybe even ways that are older than Christendom)? Or can penal substitution be rescued from its Christendom context and recalibrated for post-Christendom?

As we ponder this question, it is worth recalling that Christians in pre-Christendom (the first three centuries of church history) also attempted to tell the story of Jesus in ways that were congruent with the tradition they had inherited and meaningful to their culture. Although post-Christendom is not pre-Christendom, it has in some respects more in common with this early period than with the long Christendom period. How did the early Christians explain the death of Jesus? What model of the atonement was influential in pre-Christendom? What can we learn from this?

For nearly three hundred years after the death and resurrection of Jesus, Christians were on the social margins. They were multiplying and spreading across the ancient world, but they were a powerless and counter-cultural community, which every so often the authorities decided to persecute. These Christians were committed to taking Jesus

29

seriously, not only as their Saviour but also as their teacher and example. Enquirers and new converts were taught, not just the meaning of Jesus' death, but also the meaning of his life and his message. The church grew rapidly, lived distinctively and witnessed graciously. This was by no means a perfect church, but it was a church inspired by the life and message of Jesus.

Mostly, pre-Christendom Christians were uninterested in developing theories of the atonement. They knew Jesus had died to save them, they preached 'Christ crucified' and they celebrated his resurrection triumph over the spiritual and political powers that oppressed them. They drew on various New Testament images to explain atonement but did not insist on one formula or explanation – certainly not penal substitution, of which there is little trace in the early centuries. Most historians agree that the dominant pre-Christendom model was *Christus Victor*, in which Christ conquers the powers of evil and death, liberating humanity from their oppression.[11]

*Christus Victor*, rather than penal substitution, has been accorded the designation 'the classic theory of the atonement'. It made sense to Christians on the margins in pre-Christendom. Perhaps this model (or some version of it) will resonate also with Christians in post-Christendom, where we are once more on the margins and facing the challenge of following Jesus in a world we no longer control. Perhaps the end of Christendom is an opportunity to look afresh at various models of atonement in light of (but not in thrall to) a changing cultural context.

But the classic theory with its emphasis on the triumph of Jesus over dark forces and oppressive powers was less well suited to the Christendom era. Very unexpectedly, early in the fourth century, the emperor Constantine decided to become a Christian and to make Christianity the imperial religion. Taken by surprise and with little time to think through the implications, the church accepted the invitation to move from the margins to the centre. In an astonishingly short period, the church became powerful, wealthy and influential. Free from the fear of persecution, no longer a powerless and deviant minority, Christians celebrated the triumph of the Gospel over the empire.

There was, however, a price to pay for such influence. The counter-cultural life and teaching of Jesus was awkward in this new context, resulting in a century or so of doctrinal readjustment. By the end of this period, most theologians had abandoned the political, social and economic implications of how Jesus lived and had domesticated his teaching to support the new (Christian) status quo. Church leaders no longer prepared candidates for baptism by teaching them how to live in obedient discipleship to Jesus; instead they concentrated on ensuring that candidates believed precisely defined doctrine, which functioned as an instrument of social and religious control. In this new Christendom culture, the political dimension of Jesus' death – crucified by the same Roman state that had adopted Christianity – was profoundly embarrassing. *Christus Victor* was much less appealing now that Christians were no longer on the margins and a 'Christian empire' might conceivably be one of the oppressive powers from which the death of Jesus offered salvation!

In the centuries that followed, other models of atonement were propounded, although the classic creeds of the church never insisted on one particular interpretation (perhaps wisely recognising the element of mystery that no one model can fully express). But the church's cultural dominance and its association with the powerful in society made the 'satisfaction theory', which Anselm stated in the eleventh century,[12] especially appealing. Though, like all interpretations of atonement, this model drew on biblical imagery, the influence of the feudal system (and especially the offended honour of feudal lords) is not hard to detect. But this model is rather cold, even harsh, so the emergence of Abelard's more subjective and relational model of atonement as a counterpoint is hardly surprising.[13]

Penal substitution, most scholars agree, is a later development of the satisfaction theory, albeit using forensic and juridical imagery. And again, like all interpretations of atonement, this model is both rooted in biblical imagery – understood in particular ways – and deeply influenced by the cultural context within which it was developed. This context was the Christendom system, in which the church was powerful and successful but also coercive and sometimes violent. Penal substitution may have fitted comfortably into this cultural context and into the theology that undergirded the role of the church in Christendom, but this does not mean it is well suited to our very different context. Indeed, retaining this model of atonement may seriously hinder us from identifying and disavowing other aspects of the Christendom era that hinder our witness in post-Christendom.

The disintegration of Christendom encourages us to re-examine doctrinal and ethical convictions that may owe as much to the church's relationship with the state, its social position and even its unwitting absorption of pagan values as it owes to its founding story and biblical teaching. In relation to the doctrine of penal substitution we might note, for example, that:

- The association of the church primarily with the powerful and wealthy, rather than those on the margins and those oppressed by the system, required a model of atonement that did not threaten this relationship, even if it offered little good news to the poor and the victims. Penal substitution avoided awkward questions about institutional corruption and systemic injustice.
- The architecture of church buildings, the solemnity of the liturgy, the power of the clergy, the symbolism of works of art and numerous other cultural aspects of Christendom inculcated dread of a remote and vengeful God, predisposing theologians to develop theories of the atonement that fitted this context.
- The Christendom church rejected its traditional culture of peace and embraced a Christianised version of the pagan 'just war' approach. This embodied the myth of redemptive violence that underlies the penal substitution motif.
- The notion and practice of 'justice' in Christendom was mainly retributive and punitive rather than restorative, forensic rather than relational. This is apparent from the application of church discipline in the Christendom era. The doctrine of penal substitution is not viable unless post-biblical notions of justice are read back into the biblical text.[14]

If penal substitution is firmly rooted in biblical teaching, the scarcity of evidence for this model of atonement in pre-Christendom and its worrying congruity with values and practices of the Christendom era that many now find problematic need not cause too much concern. But if, as growing numbers of evangelicals and other Christians suggest, the biblical evidence is inconclusive or even contrary, we may become increasingly suspicious that the cultural and theological atmosphere of Christendom had greater influence than biblical exegesis on the formulation of this doctrine. And if, as many insist, there are serious theological and ethical problems with this model of atonement,[15] we may want to revisit alternative and older interpretations that are less dependent on Christendom assumptions and more hopeful and persuasive in a post-Christendom culture.

It may be significant that, as noted above, some of the most persistent critics of penal substitution are representatives of marginalised communities, unconvinced that this interpretation of the cross offers any challenge to the powerlessness and victimisation they experience and concerned that it may even legitimise their suffering. It may also be more than coincidental that several representatives of the Anabaptist tradition, who have for nearly five centuries dissented from the Christendom system and mindset, are equally critical of this doctrine.[16] Those on the margins are not always right, but the biblical tradition suggests we need to listen attentively to their perspectives if we are to discover the heart of God. And if the Gospel is truly 'good news to the poor' (Luke 4:18), we need to discover an interpretation of atonement that communicates hope and liberation to the abused, the victims and the sinned-against.

Furthermore, we need a model of atonement that is not only true to biblical teaching but relevant to contemporary culture. In a world threatened by religious, political and ideological divisions, and by deep mutual distrust, what understanding of the cross will equip followers of Jesus as peacemakers? In a world where retribution, revenge and the myth of redemptive violence have hugely increased suffering and insecurity, what understanding of the cross can offer alternatives to the present unimaginative and disastrous political policies and break the vicious circle?

Can penal substitution be reformulated and presented in a way that avoids the ethical and theological problems

33

many detect in this model of the atonement and offer good news in post-Christendom? Are the problems inherent in the doctrine itself or are they vestiges of Christendom infecting and distorting this interpretation of atonement that could be purged to leave a more satisfactory explanation?[17] Or is penal substitution so tainted by past presentations as to be better avoided? Is it too firmly rooted in imperial and coercive Christianity, in a church colluding with the powers rather than offering a prophetic challenge or an alternative vision of justice and peace?

As Christendom unravels, we have an opportunity to reconsider our understanding of atonement and other deeply held convictions that may be less biblical than we think and more influenced by a fading and oppressive culture than we realise. In our post-Christendom mission context perhaps we may dare to do what Christian thinkers in Christendom failed to do – develop doctrines of the atonement that will communicate effectively within our culture but also challenge its dominant values.

## Notes

1 This model of atonement is defined in other chapters of this book. See especially Northcott, Weaver, Myers and Thiessen.

2 Andrew Walls recognises the need to balance the 'indigenising' and 'pilgrim' principles. See Andrew Walls, *The Missionary Movement in Christian History* (T&T Clark, 1996), pp.7-9.

3 Most notably in Charles Hodge, *Systematic Theology Volume III* (Thomas Nelson, 1884).

4 In recent debates the following texts have been regarded as critical: Isaiah 53:6-10; John 11:50-2; Romans 1:18; 3:22-5; 5:8-9; 2 Corinthians 5:21; Galatians 3:13; Titus 2:14; Hebrews 9:11-28; 1 Peter 3:18 and 1 John 4:10.

5 Especially Augustine and, with less conviction, Justin Martyr. For a recent example with citations from patristic writers, see Gary Williams, 'Punished in our Place', *Evangelicals Now* (October 2004).

6 For a succinct summary of such critics see J. Denny Weaver, *The Nonviolent Atonement* (Eerdmans, 2001).

7 Those named by the Evangelical Alliance include James Dunn, Stephen Travis, Nigel Wright, Clark Pinnock, Robert Brow, Mark Baker, John Goldingay, J. Denny Weaver and Joel Green. Many more could be added.

8 Steve Chalke with Alan Mann, *The Lost Message of Jesus* (Zondervan, 2004).

9 See Steve Chalke, 'Redeeming the cross from death to life', pp.19-26, in this volume.

10 See further Stuart Murray, *Post-Christendom: Church and mission in a strange new world* (Paternoster, 2004).

11 See the classic exposition in Gustav Aulén, *Christus Victor: A historical study of the three main types of the idea of the atonement* (SPCK, 1931).

12 See Anselm's *Cur Deus Homo* (Griffin, Farran & Co, 1889).

13 On Abelard, see David Luscombe, *Peter Abelard* (London: Historical Association, 1979).

14 See further Christopher Marshall, *Beyond Retribution: A New Testament vision for crime, justice and punishment* (Eerdmans, 2001).

15 These include: punishing an innocent man – even a willing victim – is fundamentally unjust; biblical justice is essentially about the restoration of relationships rather than retribution; penal substitution is inherently violent and contravenes central aspects of the message of Jesus, not least his teaching on loving and forgiving enemies; penal substitution raises significant difficulties for our understanding of the Trinity and the relationship between the Father and the Son; penal substitution fails to engage adequately with structural and systemic evil; and (most significantly) if penal substitution is correct, neither the human life of Jesus nor his resurrection has much significance.

16 See Weaver, *The Nonviolent Atonement* and John Driver, *Understanding the Atonement for the Mission of the Church* (Herald Press, 1986). Several leaders in the UK Anabaptist Network are also critical of penal substitution.

17 For an impressive attempt to reformulate penal substitution to take account of various criticisms, see Christina Baxter, 'The Cursed Beloved: A reconsideration of penal substitution', in John Goldingay (ed.), *Atonement Today* (SPCK, 1995), pp.54-72. See also Nigel Wright's discussion of the issues in *The Radical Evangelical* (SPCK, 1996), pp.58-72.

# 4 The Passion and God's transforming love

## Vic Thiessen

In spite of many critical reviews, *The Passion of the Christ* has been much more popular in Britain and Ireland than some anticipated. Was it the media hype, the marketing campaign, or do people really want to see what Jesus was all about? Whichever it was, the film is still being used as a tool for evangelism and it is precisely as such that it needs to be challenged.[1] At the same time, it is important to respond positively to this renewed interest in Jesus' death, and the issues raised by Gibson's portrayal, to question inadequate views about the salvation offered in Christ that go back many centuries. This entails challenging the ideologically violent atonement images in the *The Passion* with non-violent, anti-sacrificial atonement theories such as those developed by Mennonite scholar J. Denny Weaver, who writes elsewhere in this volume.[2] What I offer here about God's transforming love is partly intended to act as an introduction to his essay.

*The Passion of the Christ* is not a bad film. Yes, the violence in the movie is inexcusably excessive, some would say almost sadomasochist, and this actually detracts from what is otherwise a rather more realistic depiction of the last hours of Jesus' life than one can find in previous films about Jesus. And yes, many scenes in the film will not make sense to anyone who is not familiar with the Gospel story. But, in general, *The Passion* is well made. And there is nothing inherently wrong with a film concentrating on the last few hours of Jesus' life: Christians *should* spend time reflecting on the suffering and death of Jesus. However, if such a film is used to introduce people to Christianity and show how Jesus saves us, then we have a major problem.

As an evangelistic tool, *The Passion* is supposed to convey how much Jesus (and, one must suppose, therefore God) loves us. He loves us so much that, though innocent, he was willing to suffer and suffer and suffer and die to save us from our many sins, to pay the penalty we deserved to pay. All we need to do is accept that Jesus' blood (and the film shows us a great deal of that blood) washed away our sins and then we are saved. I believe that Christians need to challenge this view of the atoning work of Jesus, if for no other reason than because it leaves the life, ministry and resurrection of Jesus completely out of the salvation picture.

As Ched Myers argues in his extensive treatment of the Passion story in St Mark,[3] Gibson's film provides no context for Jesus' suffering and crucifixion. By focusing entirely on Jesus' last hours, we get no sense at all of Jesus' life, no reason to think his life was necessary except as a prerequisite for his death; no reason to connect the way Jesus lived and taught to his crucifixion. Not that this is new to Christian theology. From the development of the creeds to what has become the dominant atonement theory, the life of Jesus has been neglected. Jesus lived so that he could die for us – end of story. If one accepts this particular view, then perhaps the film is right in failing to provide a context for Jesus' death.

J. Denny Weaver is among those who believe that it is time to question the adequacy of the dominant ('substitutionary') view of the atonement. He offers what he calls 'narrative *Christus Victor*' as an alternative framework of understanding. But before we look at this proposition, let us summarise some of the major theories of the atonement that have been offered across the Christian tradition.

The early church was not fixated on any one view of the atonement, as Michael Northcott points out later in this volume. The sacrificial death of Jesus was but one of many images the early Christians used to understand how Jesus saved us. The primary image of salvation, now called the *Christus Victor* or 'classic' view of atonement, revolved around the resurrection of Jesus, not his death. In very general terms, *Christus Victor* refers to Jesus' victory over the powers, his climactic defeat of evil, through his death and

37

resurrection. This may sound like a good place to start, but the specifics of how Jesus did this leave a lot to be desired. For the early church, it was all about a deal with the Devil, who had a legitimate right to our sinful souls. Since our souls were under his power, he could rightfully put us to death. If God wanted our souls back, he needed to pay a ransom. So God played a trick on the Devil. He offered the sinless Son of God as a ransom for captive humanity. Satan fell for it, thinking he could extend his power by killing the Son of God.

But Jesus could not be held by death and, in the resurrection, Jesus wrenches free of satan's grasp. Thus God wins the battle for humanity's souls by deceiving the deceiver. It's pretty obvious why many Christians throughout the centuries have had difficulty with God orchestrating this great fraud with Jesus as the bait. Still, it was in high favour for hundreds of years. Because it was linked to the idea of Jesus defeating the powers and in some way also with his victory over the evil Roman Empire (the book of Revelation has a lot to say about this), it's not hard to understand why this view became less favoured once Christianity became the official religion of the Roman Empire, and it never regained its status.

Since the fourth century, most Christians have believed what has become the dominant theory of the atonement, revolving around Jesus' sacrificial death in our place. While the origins of this theory can be found in the language of the letters of St Paul and in the writings of many early church leaders, it was not put into its classic formulation until the eleventh century by Anselm. This theory is called the satisfaction theory, or the substitution theory, or (in a certain limited sense) the 'objective' view.

Keep in mind, as I describe Anselm's theory, that ever since Christianity became the official religion of the Roman Empire, the Roman system of law (a retributive system of rewards and punishment) was how law was understood by the church, as opposed to the biblical system of covenant law, a system of grace that involved forgiveness, repentance and restoration. Also keep in mind that Anselm lived during a period dominated by the feudal system, in which a bond of honour exists between the feudal lord and vassal. Any infringement of the lord's honour is an assault upon the whole feudal system and so there must be a demand for satisfaction to restore order.

This had a direct impact on Anselm's theory, which goes like this: All humans are sinners in that they transgress God's law and thus do not render to God what is his due. Every sinner ought to make satisfaction to God, rendering back to God the honour they have taken away. The right order of the universe requires this satisfaction or repayment before God can remit sins. God's honour must be preserved at all costs, so God can't simply mercifully forgive. The satisfaction must be equal to the sin committed against God and the only adequate satisfaction in this case is the punishment of death: humans can't repay but God can't remit sins *without* repayment.

It is possible for another to pay the debt but only if that other is debt-free (sinless). If such a person were also more than human, his or her death might apply to all people. That is why God had to become human, so he could die the kind of death humans die, but innocently, so that his death could be applied to the account of all others. Thus, with the death of Jesus, God's honour is satisfied and God is able to forgive sinners. The death was 'propitiation' when our image is of the sacrificial offering to regain God's favour, and 'expiation' when it is about paying the debt for our sins.

The penal substitution theory dominant in Protestantism today is a variant of Anselm's view, and therefore, in proper terms, a second view in its own right. It says that humans must be punished for breaking God's law. Only Jesus, as a sinless human, can suffer the penalty and carry the guilt of all humanity. With Christ's death, justice is served and God's wrath is mollified. Anselm's view is called the 'objective' view (more accurately the *forensic* view) because Jesus had to remove a tangible barrier between God and us. Jesus' death accomplished that removal. We need only accept by faith that he has done this in order to appropriate its benefits.

A third significant view of the atonement was developed at roughly the same time as Anselm's by a theologian named Abelard. Abelard's theory is called the moral influence theory or the 'subjective' view of the atonement – since it concerns the psychology of persuasion rather than the forensic removal of a tangible barrier. Abelard believed, like Anselm, that the Devil had no right to the souls of humanity and so God did not have to pay him a ransom. And he agreed with Anselm that humanity could not pay any debt it owed to God. But the conclusion he drew from this was that atonement must therefore have nothing to do with paying anybody for anything. Instead, the self-sacrificing death of Jesus was God's act of supreme limitless love, the purpose of which was to revive our love for God and accept the forgiveness God has always wanted to give us. So there is no need to propitiate or appease a wrathful God, for God has always been loving and forgiving.

The problem is with us humans who have closed ourselves to God. Sin, in this view, is the distance between what God wants us to be and what we are. Each human can close that gap (the influence on our moral action) by freely responding to God's love and forgiveness. So this view is subjective because it is up to each of us to respond to God's love. Abelard's view, like Anselm's, focuses on the death of Jesus. This view has dominated in the liberal theology of the last two centuries and some emphasis has been placed on the life of Jesus as a moral example for us, but the resurrection is unnecessary, as it was for Anselm.

So there we have the three major theories of the atonement. All three, in their classic formulations, ignore the life of Jesus, seeing it as unnecessary except insofar as it was sinless. Only the *Christus Victor* theory sees the resurrection as necessary. It is also the only theory that has a corporate element. The *Christus Victor* theory, by highlighting the defeat of the powers, challenges the social order in a way that the other two, solidly entrenched in a society in which church and state were one, could not. So both Anselm and Abelard see salvation as something done for us as individuals and not involving the structures around us. Similarly, they have no real connection to the creation of a messianic community. As a Christian, and as an Anabaptist, I must therefore question the adequacy of these views of the atonement. In the case of Anselm's theory, Weaver even questions whether it has any merit at all.

Weaver begins by asking from what the satisfaction theory's atonement saves us. What we are usually told, as children, is that by dying undeservedly in our place, Jesus freed us all from the power of sin. Supposedly this atonement saves us from sin, but Weaver suggests that in this theory, Jesus' death doesn't save us from sin – it saves us from death, and not just death but, according to popular evangelical and Roman Catholic thinking, from eternal damnation in hell. And why would we die without this salvation? Because God's honour or God's law or God's wrath demand it. So we are, in effect, saved from God, from the violence that God would have to do to us if Jesus hadn't died for us. God's violence is also involved in God sending God's own innocent Son to die a tortuous death in order to save sinful humanity.

There have been many attempts to water down God's participation in Jesus' death, such as highlighting God's suffering with the Son, but the underlying presupposition remains that Jesus' death was divinely sanctioned and willed and necessary to satisfy an offended God. No matter how you interpret the satisfaction theory of the atonement, you cannot get away from the basic fact that in this theory God was the arranger and therefore author of Jesus' death. God required that death and loved us so much that God sent God's only Son to die in our place.

Weaver points out that even John 3:16 does not say this. There's no mention of dying in our place. And if one looks elsewhere in the New Testament, one can find a lot about Jesus dying *for* us, but not about Jesus dying in our place. The satisfaction theory presupposes that justice requires punishment, that a wrong deed can only be balanced by violence. So atonement is an act of violence by a God revealed through Jesus to be non-violent. But the difference between Christianity and many other religions is exactly that our God is not an angry God who needs to be appeased.[4]

Weaver claims that the satisfaction theory was developed to 'reflect the assumptions of the church that had accommodated violence'.[5] The dominance of this theory in

Christianity during the last millennium is reflected in Christian societies built around violent retributive justice systems, including capital punishment; Christian societies continuing to accept the redemptive value of violence, including wars; Christian societies built up around the concept of individualism instead of community; Christian societies built up around the concept of capitalism where the rich exploit the poor, even on a global scale, allowing evil structures to remain unchanged; Christian societies in which Jesus is held up as an example of passive submission to oppressive structures and violence; Christian societies in which the ethics of Jesus are peripheral to salvation, all we need to do is believe that the blood of Jesus has washed away our sins.[6]

Weaver suggests that these Christian ideas have nothing whatsoever in common with Anabaptist Christianity and that it is time for Anabaptists (and all Christians?) to abandon satisfaction atonement. This in no way abandons the saving work of Jesus. On the contrary, it offers the possibility of restoring the saving work of Jesus in all its fullness. For what if we had a theory that has at its centre the loving God Jesus revealed to us, the passion for peace and justice, including restorative justice, which Jesus showed us, the way of discipleship and the creation of a messianic community that Jesus modelled for us? Then people might understand when we say that we believe peace and justice and discipleship and community lie at the very heart of the Gospel, they're not add-ons we can take or leave as we choose. And what if this theory did not begin with 'Jesus came to die for us' but 'Jesus came to live for us', and included all of Jesus' life as well as his death and resurrection?[7]

Weaver has developed such a theory, which he has called 'narrative *Christus Victor*' because it is based on the old *Christus Victor* theory, though it differs from it in certain respects. If we drop the idea of God playing a trick on the Devil and see the Devil as including the spiritual dimension of those earthly structures not ruled by the reign of God (which Walter Wink calls 'the domination system'), then one can put together a theory in which Jesus defeats the Devil, or the powers, and saves us from our enslavement to those powers, through his life, death and resurrection.

In this view, adapted from Weaver, but including ideas from Walter Wink, René Girard and John Howard Yoder, Jesus came to make the Kingdom of God ('God's domination-free order', Wink) visible in the world; to be a witness to the reign of God in his person and his teaching; and to invite people to be a part of this liberating kingdom. This involved overcoming the domination system in his own life, freeing himself of its violent influence, and then confronting the domination system, challenging all the oppressive structures (like violence, exploitation of the poor, sexism, classism, racism, etc.) that run counter to the reign of God. Jesus' exposure of the oppression of the domination system resulted directly in his death at its hands.

Obviously Jesus would have anticipated such a result to his exposure of the domination system, but that does not mean he tried to get himself killed or that God *arranged* for him to die that way, for his death was not *needed* or desired by God to balance a cosmic equation. But the death of Jesus *did* further expose the illegitimacy of the domination system, for it was the law, the place where people looked for good, that killed him, thus exposing the law, and the whole way of living that violence defends, as an attack against God. And, by submitting to the evil of the violent powers rather than meeting it on its own terms, Jesus *did* reveal that the reign of God does not respond to violence with violence (*The Passion of the Christ* does well in showing Jesus' loving response to the violence being done to him).

By killing Jesus, the powers thought they had eliminated the problem, but their violence against Jesus failed to deflect his challenges or his way. And the resurrection revealed that it is the reign of God and not the domination system that is the ultimate power, and shaper of reality, in the universe;[8] it vindicated the way of Jesus. The resurrection is the definitive victory of the reign of God over the forces of evil.

In this theory, salvation can be found in each part of Jesus' life, death and resurrection. Jesus saved us through his life by showing us what the reign of God looks like, how to be free from the domination system and expose it, and how to live a life of compassion. When we follow Jesus, living like him in the presence of the reign of God and witnessing to that reign, we are defeating the Devil and participating in salvation. Jesus saved us through his death by showing us the consequences of such a life, how to meet death without violence or fear, and by further exposing the failures and evil of the domination system.

And last, but by no means least, we are saved by the resurrection, which assures us that the powers have already been defeated, that the violence of death has been overcome and the reign of God is at hand. In light of the resurrection, we can witness to this reign of God in confidence, knowing that the delusion of the domination system's ultimate weapon of violence, death, has been shattered. Death is impotent against the power of love.

This view of the atonement not only challenges the oppressive structures around us; it challenges each of us and our complicity with those structures. We need to confess and repent as a response to the forgiveness offered by a merciful and loving God, who invites us to join the reign of God even though we have participated with the powers of evil that killed Jesus. Repentance is costly, for it involves a transformed life that confronts oppression and continues the work of Jesus in making the reign of God, a new understanding of reality, present and visible on earth. This may include suffering, as it did for Jesus, but we know that God will be suffering with us, as God suffered with Jesus. And we are not to walk this path alone but in the context of a distinct inclusive voluntary community living a new way of life (Yoder).

Many people have challenged various aspects of Weaver's 'narrative *Christus Victor*' theory. Some have questioned Weaver's formulation of another 'totalising' theory, especially a theory that neglects other non-violent biblical motifs. While I sympathise with Weaver's 'narrative *Christus Victor*', I would agree that there might be room to incorporate other non-violent motifs (e.g. reworking Abelard's theory to include corporate and structural elements) into our understanding of Jesus' salvific work.

Scholars such as Chris Marshall (who is involved in the Anabaptist Association of Australia and New Zealand) have pointed to the many biblical statements that would indicate the necessity of Jesus' death for our salvation and also that God willed that death. Marshall agrees with Weaver that Jesus' death is not about violent satisfaction atonement, but argues that Jesus' death was necessary to break the cycle of violence – by enduring 'the supreme violence of an unjust execution without seeking or desiring retaliation . . . In so doing Jesus broke the mimetic or payback mechanism that lies at the heart of sin's power (something beyond the reach of any display of coercive power, even God's power) and unleashed the liberative power of forgiveness.'[9]

Marshall argues against Weaver that this was God's will and purpose in sending God's Son into the world. While I agree that the New Testament makes such claims, I would suggest we need, first, to define what we mean by God's will and purpose (could God *will* Jesus' death on the cross without somehow *willing* the authorities to kill him?); second, to ask whether a non-violent Jesus revealed a non-violent God; and, third, to ask whether it is possible that such claims may be misleading. These are major issues that we, as Anabaptists, need to deal with if our understanding of the Gospel of Jesus is to have integrity in our postmodern world. Wrestling with J. Denny Weaver's nonviolent atonement and non-violent God is a step forward on that path.

*The Passion*, on the other hand, is, overall, a step backward. It provides no reasons for the death of Jesus and portrays the crucifixion as a violent spiritual experience between God, the Son and the Devil. This might reveal how much God loved us but doesn't say much about how we are to live our lives or how we are to live in a world full of violence, war, poverty and oppression. Despite the accusations of anti-Semitism (the film is no more anti-Semitic than some of the gospels), the film does not make clear who is to blame for Jesus' death. It doesn't suggest, as Weaver and Fraser do, that we are all complicit in the horrific suffering and death of Jesus when we fail to follow Jesus in challenging the powers; when we continue to live in a world where a few (we) live in luxury while countless millions suffer under oppression and poverty, without act-

ing daily to change that world and witness to the reign of
God.

## Notes

1 An analysis has recently been published of the evangelistic use of
  Gibson's *The Passion of the Christ*, though it largely by-passes the critical
  questions raised in this book. See: Martin Thompson, *The Impact of The
  Passion of the Christ in Churches in England and Wales* (Bible Society,
  December 2004).
2 See J. Denny Weaver, 'Jesus' death and the non-violent victory of God',
  in this volume, pp.47-59.
3 See Ched Myers, 'The Gospel of the cross confronts the powers', in this
  volume, pp.61-73.
4 J. Denny Weaver, *The Nonviolent Atonement* (Grand Rapids: Eerdmans,
  2001).
5 Weaver, *The Nonviolent Atonement*, p.97.
6 See Weaver, *The Nonviolent Atonement*.
7 See Weaver, *The Nonviolent Atonement*.
8 Weaver, *The Nonviolent Atonement*, p.211.
9 Christopher D. Marshall, 'Atonement, Violence and the Will of God: A
  sympathetic response to J. Denny Weaver's *The Nonviolent Atonement*',
  *Mennonite Quarterly Review*, January, 2003, p.91.

# 5 Jesus' death and the non-violent victory of God

## J. Denny Weaver

Questions of violence and atonement have generated much discussion in the last several years. I make a two-fold argument about atonement and violence. One side of the argument is the contention that all images of atonement as we have come to understand them have violent problematic dimensions that render them unacceptable. My argument has a sharp edge to it. Counter to a common methodology of trying to salvage all atonement motifs and integrate them into a larger, supposedly more complete picture of the significance of the death of Jesus, I have argued that satisfaction atonement, in *any* of its forms, is intrinsically violent and should be abandoned.[1]

The other side of the argument, pursued here, is to construct an alternative motif that is thoroughly non-violent and that avoids the errors and problems discernible in satisfaction atonement. This constructive task is broad, ranging from Genesis to Revelation. It is actually more than an atonement motif. It is a way of reading the entire biblical story, as well as the history of atonement doctrine, with implications far beyond atonement.

The standard account of the history of doctrine lists three families of atonement images. These are *Christus Victor* (including some version of 'ransom' theory whereby people are captive to the Devil, or God is waging a cosmic battle against the Evil One), 'satisfaction' theories (in several versions, most notably Anselm's theory that Jesus' death was necessary in order to satisfy the honour of God, which had been irreparably offended by ·sin), and the 'moral influence' idea, whereby God the Father moves us sinners to love by giving us his most precious possession, his Son, to die for us. Vic Thiessen has outlined these in his chapter of this volume, and a number of the other contributors make critiques of their assumptions. There is much to say about the different theories, and I have indeed unpacked and responded to them in some detail in my books *The Nonviolent Atonment* and *Keeping Salvation Ethical*.

For example, it is not difficult to see that Anselm's image of the atoning death of Jesus reflects the feudal world-view. Human sin has brought imbalance and disharmony into the universe. The restoration of harmony, order and balance requires a payment to satisfy the offended honour of God. Anselm understood Jesus' death as the debt payment that satisfied the honour of God, and thus restored balance and order in the universe. The logic of satisfaction atonement can be understood with all the feudal imagery removed from Anselm's argument. For example, the modern criminal justice system constitutes an arena that assumes and models retribution. As at least one major historian has shown, feudal society supplies the motif that Anselm elevated to an ultimate image of the way that God maintains order in the universe.[2] Maintaining order in the universe depends on maintaining the honour of God, which necessitates a debt payment – the death of Jesus – to cover the offence to God's honour that was enacted by human sin.

Although Anselm's understanding of satisfaction atonement differs significantly from penal substitutionary atonement, I view them as belonging together, as two versions of atonement that depict a divine need for Jesus' death. In different ways, each depends on retribution. Any and all versions of satisfaction atonement, regardless of their packaging, assume the violence of retribution or justice based on punishment, and depend on God-induced and God-directed violence.

Satisfaction atonement accommodates violence by structuring the relationship between humankind and God in terms of an ahistorical, abstract legal formula. Thus it concerns a relationship that is outside of human history. Further, when visualising the birth, life and teaching, death and resurrection of Jesus, quite obviously satisfaction atonement actually needs or uses only the death of Jesus. These elements – positing a transaction outside of history and involving only the death of Jesus – make satisfaction atonement an image that (with one exception treated below) implies little or nothing about ethics, and contains nothing that would challenge injustice in the social order. It is an a-ethical atonement image – it projects an understanding of salvation that is separated from ethics. That is, salvation in satisfaction atonement does not envision a change of status in history or in life on earth; rather it envisions a change in one's status outside of or beyond this life. This a-ethical orientation makes it quite compatible with exercise of the sword, or with accommodation of slavery and racism.

In addition to arguments about the inner logic of the satisfaction atonement formulas and the image of God they portray, it is also important to examine the image and role of Jesus in these formulas. The importance of this question appears when Jesus is accepted as a reference point for ethics – whether one thinks in terms of the quickly recited 'What would Jesus do?' to very profound discussions of discipleship.

In satisfaction atonement, Jesus is a model of voluntary submission to innocent suffering. Since the Father needs the death of Jesus to satisfy divine honour, Jesus voluntarily agrees to submit to that violence needed to satisfy the honour of God. Or Jesus voluntarily agrees to undergo the punishment deserved by sinful humankind in order that the demand of divine justice is met. In either case, Jesus is a passive and innocent victim, and his role was to submit to that unjust suffering. Because Jesus' death is needed, Jesus models being a voluntary, passive and innocent victim, who submits to suffering for the good of another.

It is important to underscore for whom these images of Jesus as an innocent and passive victim may pose a particular concern. As Brown, Parker, Brock and others have pointed out, it is an unhealthy model for a woman abused by her husband or a child violated by her father, and constitutes double jeopardy when attached to hierarchical theology that asserts male headship.[3] A model of passive, innocent suffering poses an obstacle for people who

49

encounter conditions of systemic injustice, or an unjust status quo produced by the power structure. A short list of examples includes: the legally segregated South prior to the civil rights movement; the de facto housing segregation that still exists in many places; and military-backed occupation, under which land is confiscated and indigenous residents crowded into enclosed territories, called 'reservations' in North America, 'bantustans' in South Africa and 'autonomous areas' in Palestine. For people in such situations of an unjust status quo, the idea of 'being like Jesus' as modelled by satisfaction atonement means to submit passively and to endure that systemic injustice.

James Cone linked substitutionary atonement specifically to defences of slavery and colonial oppression.[4] Delores Williams calls the Jesus of substitutionary atonement, the 'ultimate surrogate figure', which would validate all the unjust surrogacy roles to which black women have been and still are subjected.[5] Such examples show that atonement theology that models innocent, passive suffering does have specific negative impact in the contemporary context.[6]

A victim is controlled by forces and circumstances beyond himself or herself. A victim surrenders control to others and accepts the injustice imposed by others. Jesus, in satisfaction and substitutionary atonement, models victimisation. When this atonement motif is the model for people who have experienced abuse or exploitation, this model underscores their status as victims. For them, being like Jesus means to continue to submit to unjust suffering, abuse or exploitation. And it should be obvious that since satisfaction poses an image of submission to oppression, it poses no specific challenge to the acts of those who oppress and exploit.

As previous authors in this volume have pointed out, emphasising the passivity in Jesus' atoning work points to another problem with satisfaction atonement. That problem is that it focuses on Jesus' death as the culmination and high point of his life, and with the focus on his death, that particular moment becomes the moment that defines his work.

For one, if Jesus' death is the purpose and culmination of

his existence, then his life and teaching are rendered peripheral to the task of providing the death required by divine honour or divine law. As was the case with Anselm's *Cur Deus Homo*, it is in fact possible to discuss the saving work of Jesus without mentioning any specifics of his life or teaching at all. Stated another way, the effect if not the intent of focus on Jesus' death as the saving element of his work is to relegate his life (along with his teaching) to an elaborate means of getting him killed, so that the death can fly Godward to satisfy divine honour or divine law.

Considering and valuing Jesus' death apart from the story of his life also contributes in a major way to portraying it as passive submission to innocent suffering. His death appears much less passive when examined as one particular incident in the context of the entire scope of his life, including his resurrection. In fact, as the story is told in the gospels, his life is assertive and confrontational. He announced his mission as one 'to bring good news to the poor . . . to proclaim release to the captives and recovery of sight to the blind, to let the oppressed go free' (Luke 4:18). That is an active, not a passive, mission.

In Walter Wink's interpretation of Jesus' well-known statements about turning the other cheek, giving the cloak, and going the second mile, these admonitions are actually activist, non-violent resistance strategies rather than injunctions to passive submission as usually interpreted.[7] Past the Sermon on the Mount, there are stories which show Jesus in conversation with women when that is not expected – in these instances he is challenging some accepted conventions, and thus raising the status of women. His stories confront the racism against Samaritans by raising their status. Jesus' teachings show concern for poor people. Many such stories could be recounted in detail.

Luke 6:6-11 has a story about Jesus healing a withered hand. A dominant feature of the story is that the healing occurred on the Sabbath day, which was a defiance of the conventional expectations. And the defiance of expectations was clearly deliberate – Jesus had the man come to a prominent spot where everyone could see him, and he looked 'around at all of them', evidently making eye contact and drawing their eyes to him, before he acted. Other stories in the gospels have similar features. Jesus made the authorities so mad that they started plotting how to kill him.

When the death of Jesus is pictured in the light of his life, it appears that death is not the culmination. His mission was to make the reign of God visible, which is visible and present in his person and in his teaching and in his life, his acts. Thus the incarnation itself has an activist agenda – to make God's reign present and visible in our history. Seen in this light, the death of Jesus – the cross – is neither the goal nor the culmination of the story. Jesus' death is the result of faithfully carrying out his mission of making God's rule present in the world. His death was not something desired by God to balance a cosmic equation. Rather it was willed by the forces that were threatened by the presence of the reign of God in our history. The passive image of the death of Jesus actually contradicts the activist purpose of the incarnation, God coming to us in and as Jesus of Nazareth.

Of course, none of this discussion about violence and the image of God in atonement motifs and about Jesus as passive model of innocent suffering matters *if* Jesus' life is not related to what it means to be a Christian, and *if* being saved is a status separated from ethics. On the other hand, *if* the life of Jesus is relevant as a norm for ethics and *if* being saved and being Christian have implications for ethics, then the discussion of the image of God and violence in Christian atonement motifs and the image of Jesus as passive model of innocent suffering have profound importance.

If we take Jesus seriously as a model and a norm for Christians, and if in his person and in his life Jesus is the presence of the reign of God in our history (this is a statement of incarnation), then how we understand atonement is an image of how God works in the world and how we understand what it means to be a Christian in the world. Satisfaction atonement in any of its forms pictures God as a God whose modus operandi in the world is retributive violence and it presents an image of Jesus that models passive, innocent submission to abuse and oppression. I

believe that this image of God and this image of atonement, and the image of being a Christian in the world that
they present, should be abandoned. Obviously, that conclusion raises a big question. What would I put in its place?
I have a suggestion, which can be only sketched here.

Revelation 12 features the specific image of a heavenly
battle between the forces of satan, represented by the
dragon, and the forces of God led by the angel Michael.
This battle follows the birth of a baby who was snatched up
to heaven after the dragon tried unsuccessfully to kill him.
The image of the baby snatched up to heaven clearly refers
to the death and resurrection of Jesus, which means that
the woman with a crown of twelve stars is Israel that produced Jesus and then the church. The dragon is called 'the
devil and Satan' (Revelation 12:9), but the seven heads and
ten horns and seven crowns identify it as a symbol of
Rome. There is here then an image of the reign of God in
the person of Jesus confronting the evil of the world, symbolised by Rome, a confrontation which is continued by the
life of the church. The so-called cosmic battle is really
imagery that gives the cosmic significance of the confrontation in history between the Roman Empire and Jesus
and his church – what I called narrative *Christus Victor*. The
same kind of interpretation applies to the seven seals in
chapters 6 and 7, and can be developed throughout the
entire book of Revelation.[8]

Of particular importance is the observation that the victory of the reign of God over the evil symbolised by Rome
occurs *non-violently*, through the life, death and most
significantly the resurrection of Jesus and through the
witness of the church, which maintains its witness in
the face of adversity and death. That victory through the
resurrection is obvious in the vignettes of the seals in
Revelation 6-7 and the heavenly battle of chapter 12. But it
bears pointing out specifically for the image of the rider on
the white horse in chapter 19, which is often appealed to in
order to show the supposed violence of God and the ultimately vengeful and violent attitude of God toward evil. I
simply note that the rider's robe is dipped in blood *before*
the supposed battle, and that his name is 'the Word of God'

(Revelation 19:13), which clearly identify the rider as the resurrected Jesus.

Then note that there is no actual battle depicted; rather the armies of the kings of the earth are defeated by the sword that extends from his mouth (Revelation 19:21), which makes it the Word of God and not violence that defeats evil. Ephesians 6:17 and Hebrews 4:12 also used a two-edged sword for the Word of God. The important point to note is that the graphic image of the rider on a white horse is not about violence at all. It is another statement that in the resurrection of Jesus, the reign of God conquers evil, and that victory occurs non-violently, through resurrection.

The gospels present the same story as that told in Revelation, but from a different standpoint. Revelation tells the story of Jesus from the perspective of the heavenly throne room and the future culmination of the reign of God. The gospels narrate that same story from the earthly vantage point of the folks who got dust on their sandals as they walked along the roads of Palestine with Jesus. Both the gospels and Revelation locate the victory of the reign of God on earth and in history – narrative *Christus Victor* – and make quite clear that the triumph occurred not through the sword and military might but non-violently, through death and resurrection. The intrinsically non-violent character of the victory eliminates what is usually called triumphalism of the church. As intrinsically non-violent, its stance to the other or toward those who differ and are different can only be non-violent. To be otherwise is to cease to be a witness to the reign of God and to join the forces of evil who oppose the reign of God.

At the same time, reading that story in the gospels shows that Jesus was not a passive victim, whose purpose was to get himself killed in order to satisfy a big cosmic legal requirement. Rather, Jesus was an activist, whose mission was to make the rule of God visible. And as was suggested above, his acts demonstrated what the reign of God looked like – defending poor people, raising the status of women, raising the status of Samaritans, performing healings and exorcisms, preaching the reign of God, and more. His mission was an activist mission to make the reign of God present in the world in his person and in his teaching, and to invite people to experience the liberation it presented.

And when Jesus made the reign of God visible and present in that way, it was so threatening that the assembled array of evil forces killed him. These forces include imperial Rome, which carried ultimate legal authority for his death, with some assistance from the religious authorities in Jerusalem, as well as Judas, Peter and other disciples, who could not even watch with him, and the mob that howled for his death. Resurrection is the reign of God made victorious over all these forces of evil that killed Jesus.

As sinners, in one way or another, we are all part of those sinful forces that killed Jesus.[9] Jesus died making the reign of God present for us while we were still sinners. To acknowledge our human sinfulness is to become aware of our participation in the forces of evil that killed Jesus, including their present manifestations in such powers as militarism, nationalism, racism, sexism, heterosexism and poverty that still bind and oppress.

And because God is a loving God, God invites us to join the rule of God in spite of the fact that we participated with and are captive to the powers that killed Jesus. We cannot compensate for nor make up for our participation with the powers that killed Jesus. But the marvellous thing is that God invites us to participate in the reign of God anyway. That is what grace is. That participation in the reign of God in spite of our guilt for opposing the reign of God is grace. It is also grace because under our own power, we cannot resist and overcome the powers of evil. Only God can do that, and if we are resisting and overcoming, it is because God enables it. Call that predestination if you wish. At the same time, we are not robots and we have to make a choice whether to remain in league with the forces that oppose God or to cease rebellion and to accept God's invitation and to join with the reign of God. Call that free will or Arminianism if you wish.

God invites us to join the struggle of those seeking liberation from the forces that bind and oppress. This invitation envisions both those who are oppressed and their oppressors. When the oppressed accept God's invitation, they cease collaborating with the powers that oppressed and join the forces who represent the reign of God in making a visible witness against oppression. Although they may still suffer as a result of the struggle, they have ceased being victims who submit willingly to unjust suffering. And when the oppressors accept God's invitation, they cease their collaboration with the powers of oppression, and join the forces who represent the reign of God in witnessing against oppression. Thus under the reign of God, former oppressed and former oppressors join together in witnessing to the reign of God.[10]

Earlier it was indicated how Anselmian atonement correlates with the ecclesiology of Christendom. It is now also possible to say that narrative *Christus Victor* belonged to, and in fact only makes sense when perceived within, the ecclesiological status of the early church in relation to the Roman Empire and the social order. As is clear from the symbolism of Revelation, the church in that setting perceived itself to be different from the empire, to maintain itself as distinct from the prevailing social order. My reconstruction of narrative *Christus Victor* that makes visible the church in Revelation and the life of Jesus in the gospels simply reflects the status of the church in the first century and beyond. I note without elaboration that this church was a pacifist church, whether that stance was because Christians did not wield the sword and shed blood or because of the idolatrous nature of the army's religious commitments.[11]

It was this sense of being distinct from the social order that disappeared with the Constantinian synthesis. And with that accommodation, historical dimensions of narrative *Christus Victor* were no longer true, and cosmic imagery did not match the political reality. Thus eventually the motif I have called narrative *Christus Victor* could fade away without a sense of loss, to be replaced by Anselm's satisfaction motif, which reflected the medieval social and ecclesiological conditions.

The image of narrative *Christus Victor* avoids all the problematic elements in classic atonement images, particularly those of satisfaction atonement. It is grounded in assumptions of non-violence – the non-violence of Jesus –

rather than violence. In particular, it does not assume retribution, or the assumption that injustice is balanced by the violence of punishment. It does not put God in the role of chief avenger, nor picture God as a child abuser. And it is abundantly obvious that God did not need the death of Jesus.

To depict the reign of God as made visible by Jesus, and to depict its non-violent dimension, it is necessary to make use of the entire life and teaching of Jesus, rather than focus only on his death. When this mission threatens the forces of evil, they retaliate with violence, killing Jesus. This suffering is not something willed by nor needed by God and it is not directed Godward. On the contrary, the killing of Jesus is the ultimate contrast between the non-violent reign of God and the rule of evil.

Jesus does suffer and die, but suffering and dying were not the purpose and the goal of his life and mission. It is not as an act of passive submission to undeserved suffering. Death resulted when Jesus carried out his mission to make the rule of God present and visible. This was a mission that sought life and liberation from oppression. Death was a by-product of this life-giving and life-bringing mission. To understand how death was a by-product rather than the goal of his actions, recall the murders of Martin Luther King, Jr and Archbishop Romero. These men were killed because of their work, but getting killed was in no way the purpose of their work.

I want to make very clear here that I am not denying that Jesus was killed, nor am I removing his death from the Gospel story. What I am doing is developing a different understanding of the role of Jesus' death in the discussion of the story of salvation. I am arguing that death is not something that was willed or needed by God. Death does not pay off or satisfy anything. On the contrary, it is a product of the forces of evil that opposed Jesus and opposed the reign of God. The real saving act of and in and with Jesus is his resurrection.

Narrative *Christus Victor* understands Jesus as the one whose person and mission make the reign of God present in our history. It pictures Jesus with an activist mission, as a model of liberation. Those who accept the invitation of

God join the movement that witnesses to the nature of the reign of God in contrast to the forces of evil that bind. This motif thus features salvation that begins in history to the extent that the reign of God is present in history.

Earlier, one of the questions used to analyse the various atonement motifs was 'Who needs the death of Jesus?' Bringing that question to narrative *Christus Victor* brings to the forefront the profound difference between it and satisfaction atonement. The question has a non-answer in narrative *Christus Victor*. God does not need the death because this motif does not make use of the idea of retribution. In narrative *Christus Victor*, the death pays God nothing and is not Godward directed. The death of Jesus is thus very pointedly not something needed by God or God's honour. It is rather what the forces of evil – 'the Devil' – do to Jesus. Rather than a divine requirement, the death of Jesus is the ultimate indication of the difference between the reign of God and the reign of evil.

Rather than the death of Jesus, what sinners need, what the reign of God needs, is the resurrection of Jesus. That is where the victory of the reign of God is. And this discussion shows one of the most profound differences between satisfaction atonement and narrative *Christus Victor*. Satisfaction atonement focuses on the death of Jesus, and uses and needs that death. And satisfaction atonement has God arrange things so that the death happens in order to satisfy the divine requirement. And it does not even talk about resurrection. Whereas for narrative *Christus Victor*, death has an entirely different meaning. The death of Jesus is not a divine requirement. Rather, the death is that which clearly distinguishes the rule of the Devil from the rule of God. The rule of the Devil attempts to rule by violence and death, whereas the rule of God rules and ultimately conquers by non-violence.

The analysis in this chapter has demonstrated the extent to which presuppositions of violence as well as overt violence are inherently a part of supposed standard Christian theology. We have also observed that the abstract and ahistorical character of the classic formulas of atonement mean that they accommodate violence and do not challenge injustice in the social order. This combination of intrinsically violent elements and lack of challenge to injustice in the social order mean that it has been possible throughout much of Christian history for Christians to profess allegiance to Jesus and to claim salvation as depicted in classic Christology and atonement, while simultaneously pursuing the violence prohibited by Jesus' teaching and life.

If Christians are uncomfortable with Christianity as a violent religion – and of late there seem to be many supposedly Christian voices joining the national war chorus – the first step is to recognise the extent to which formulas of classic theology have contributed to violence both overt and systemic. This paper provides some data for that acknowledgement. The second step away from Christianity as a violent religion would be to construct theology that specifically reflects the non-violence of its namesake, Jesus Christ. As a suggestion in that direction, I offer narrative *Christus Victor* as both non-violent atonement and narrative Christology. Finally, step three would be to live out the theology of its non-violent namesake. That commitment is a call to every Christian.

## Notes

1 This is an edited down and adapted version (by Simon Barrow) of a paper first given at the European Mennonite Theology Forum, held in England and organised by the London Mennonite Centre, in March 2004. Both the author and the editor gave papers at this event.

2 R. W. Southern, *Saint Anselm: A portrait in a landscape* (Cambridge University Press, 1990), pp.221-7.

3 Joanne Carlson Brown and Rebecca Parker, 'For God So Loved the World?', in *Christianity, Patriarchy and Abuse: A feminist critique*, edited by Joanne Carlson Brown and Carole R. Bohn (Pilgrim Press, 1989); Julie M. Hopkins, *Towards a Feminist Christology: Jesus of Nazareth, European women and the Christological crisis* (Eerdmans, 1995), pp.50-2; Rita Nakashima Brock, *Journeys by Heart: A Christology of erotic power* (Crossroad, 1988), pp.55-7; Carter Heyward, *Saving Jesus From Those Who Are Right: Rethinking what it means to be Christian* (Fortress Press, 1999), p.151.

4 James H. Cone, *God of the Oppressed* (SPCK, 1977), pp.211-2.

5 Delores S. Williams, *Sisters in the Wilderness: The challenge of womanist God-talk* (Orbis Books, 1993), pp.60-83, 161-7, 178-99.

6 One of the most explicit examples of innocent suffering for another is the vocation of 'victim soul', which was a prominent feature of some

Catholic religious Orders, primarily for women, in the nineteenth and well into the twentieth century. See Paula M. Kane, 'She Offered Herself Up: The victim soul and victim spirituality in Catholicism', *Church History* 71, no. 1 (March 2002), pp.80-120.

7 Walter Wink, *Engaging the Powers: Discernment and resistance in a world of domination*, vol. 3 (Fortress Press, 1992), pp.175-84.

8 See J. Denny Weaver, *The Nonviolent Atonement* (Eerdmans, 2001), pp.20-8.

9 See James Carroll, *Constantine's Sword: The Church and the Jews: A history* (Houghton Mifflin Company, 2001), pp.71-88, 175-6.

10 This is an image of narrative *Christus Victor*, using the book of Revelation and the gospels. For a much fuller development, as well as for discussion of how it fits with Paul and other literature of the New Testament, see my *The Nonviolent Atonement* (Eerdmans, 2001).

11 David G. Hunter, 'The Christian Church and the Roman Army in the First Three Centuries', in *The Church's Peace Witness*, edited by Marlin E. Miller and Barbara Nelson Gingerich (Eerdmans, 1994), pp.161-81; David G. Hunter, 'A Decade of Research on Early Christians and Military Service', *Religious Studies Review* 18, no. 2 (April 1992), pp.87-94; David M. Scholer, 'Early Christian Attitudes to War and Military Service: A Selective Bibliography', *TSF Bulletin* 8, no. 1 (September-October 1984), pp.23-4.

# 6 The Gospel of the cross confronts the powers

## Ched Myers

The most concise thing I can say about my reaction to Mel Gibson's *The Passion of the Christ* is: I loved the book, but hated the movie. There is much to be perplexed and/or enraged about in Gibson's cinematic version of the trial and execution of Jesus. And there is plenty to deconstruct concerning the film-maker and his psyche, not least his fascination for *Braveheart*-type victim-heroes who suffer injustice and indignity, but ultimately wreak righteous and intensely violent payback on their adversaries. But the public issue most stimulated by the film has been whether or not it would rekindle old and persistent embers of anti-Semitism, and that is far more important to address than Gibson and his theology.

More than any of his particular characterisations, the thing that makes Gibson's work a potential tool for anti-Semitism is the structure of his story as a whole. He has chosen to make an account of a political trial and execution without ever bothering to explain why that confrontation occurred. The inevitable result of narrating the death of Jesus without narrating his life is that the credulous viewer is forced to surmise that Jesus must have been a nice guy who was killed for no good reason by mean, spiteful people. And if in addition the theological assumption (as is the case for Gibson) is that the main purpose of Jesus' life was for him to die 'for our sins', then someone had to do the dirty deed of killing him. Why not scapegoat 'the Jews' as a whole? It makes a perfect rationale for Christian supercessionism.

Such an interpretation of the Jesus story is, of course, a classic expression of Doceticism, the earliest Christian

61

heresy (in which Jesus is seen as divine but not fully human). The early church roundly condemned it, but we might say the church won that battle but lost the war, for Docetic Christologies have functionally prevailed for most of the post-Constantinian history of Christianity. And when it comes to the matter of Jesus' trial and death, they have had horrific historical consequences.

The Judean authorities that we meet in the gospels are portrayed as political officials conspiring to remove a dissident they perceive to be a threat to the status quo. This may be an ugly little scenario, but it is certainly not an uncommon one; one can find analogies throughout the history of civilisation, from Socrates to Martin Luther King. But once these Judean authorities are portrayed by interpreters of the gospel as the uniquely fated villains in a cosmic drama, the storyline inevitably becomes conflated into 'Jews are Christ-killers.'

And let us be clear: readings of the Gospel that blame 'the Jews' and exonerate the Romans for Jesus' demise are still prevalent throughout Christendom, and Gibson's film has done nothing to resist or even acknowledge their terrible potential. This tradition has fuelled two dark legacies through the ages. One is anti-Semitism, in all its different epochal guises. But the other is a fantasy nurtured within Christendom that apprehends imperial authority as benign or even beneficent. It is a (mis)perception from which the current American empire continues to benefit. In these ways, then, narratives like Gibson's perpetuate a version of Jesus' 'life-less death' that is truly death-dealing rather than life-giving. As René Girard and his followers have long argued, the myth of redemptive violence empowers not redemption, but only more violence.

Gibson has made the claim – at once both presumptuous and duplicitous – that any 'problems' his critics may have lie not with the film, but with the gospels themselves. And indeed the question has been raised afresh in the wake of the movie. Many liberals, both secular and religious, are responding by stipulating in various ways that the gospel sources are neither historically credible nor even theologically reliable.

It took a thoughtful rabbi to point out the obvious: It is

unproductive for liberal theologians to criticise *The Passion* on the grounds that it is not consistent with what scholars now know of the historical accuracy of the gospel accounts. Fundamentalists and traditionalists are not concerned with the 'historical Jesus' or trying to discover Jesus the Jew. That has been an exercise for liberal Christian and Jewish scholars studying the Second Temple time period. In my opinion a better approach, and one with at least some chance of engaging conservatives who don't try to solve problems by throwing out the ancient texts, is to offer a careful alternative reading of those texts.

The best defence against bad theology and bad politics is a more rigorous and compelling handling of the text. I therefore wish to offer an alternative reading of the gospel narrative of the arrest, trial and death of Jesus that takes seriously the legacy of anti-Semitic hermeneutics, but which also preserves the integrity and reliability of the scriptural texts.

There can be no question that the gospel accounts of Jesus' death are fiercely critical in their portraits of the Judean authorities. This *in itself*, however, does not make them anti-Semitic. But it certainly *is* the case that when wrenched out of context, these gospel criticisms can be and have been used to legitimate an anti-Semitic ideology. Given this history of abuse in Christendom, one cannot simply exonerate the texts by insisting that they be separated from the history of their (mis)interpretation. One must rather feel the weight of this toxic legacy, and label these texts as one might a box of potent drugs which can both heal and kill: 'Handle with care.'

One of the many problems with Gibson's film is that it weaves in strands from all four of our gospel versions (not to mention his own gratuitous additions). Attempts to 'harmonise' what are four very different versions of the Jesus story have long been discredited because they give the editor such wide license to pick and choose. This effectively creates a 'fifth' gospel – or in Gibson's case, anti-gospel. To sort these matters out we must first remember that every historical narrative (ancient or modern) is an ideological product. Thus it is the gospel writer's ideology – reflected in the way he has shaped, coloured and exaggerated events

63

and characters – that holds the key to whatever historical knowledge we can glean from these ancient testimonies.

Careful literary analysis of Mark reveals it as a powerful parody of the political–legal process that condemned the prophet Jesus. This 'fiction', understood within the historical and social context in which it was produced, reflects an even-handed critique of the Judean and Roman authorities, indeed portrays their collusion. Moreover, it articulates a sophisticated political theology which understands that resistance to injustice will inevitably bring confrontation with 'the Powers'. But it also believes that non-violent witness will ultimately prevail over opportunistic politics and brute force.

Mark's account of the trial of Jesus is found in Mark 14:43–15:20. It takes place in the span of twenty-four hours, and is peppered by a refrain of public mockery. Jesus is ridiculed first by the Judean security forces (14:65), then by the Roman soldiers (15:16-20), and finally by the crowd gathered at the cross (15:29-32). Each refrain functions in Mark's narrative strategy as ironic confirmation of Jesus' stature as 'prophet', 'king' and finally 'Messiah'.

Let us begin where Gibson's film starts: in the Garden of Gethsemane. Mark's portrayal of Jesus' seizure by the Judean authorities reeks of the overkill so typical of covert government action against civilian dissidents: a secret signal, a surprise attack at night, the heavily armed contingent (Mark 14:43-52). This all suggests that the security squad expected armed resistance; we are told that their instructions are to take Jesus away under 'heavy guard' (Greek *asphaloos*). Mark uses the brief skirmish that ensues (14:47) as an occasion for Jesus to point out the sordid character of the whole operation, holding the attackers responsible for the violence.

'Have you come to capture me with swords and clubs as if I was a robber?' Jesus asks with dry sarcasm (14:48). The Greek verb *sullambanoo* (rather than the more common *krateoo*) is probably a biblical allusion to the arrest of the prophet Jeremiah (Jeremiah 37:14). We also encounter here the Greek noun *leesteen* for the first time in Mark. We know from Josephus that this term was used to describe 'social bandits', a broad rubric that included nationalist Jewish guerrillas, Robin-hood-type rural insurgents and urban terrorists. Jesus will be executed by the Romans between two such 'robbers' (Mark 15:27). By using this term Mark is contending that both Judean and Roman authorities apprehended Jesus as an insurrectionist. If modern readers (or film-makers) wish to ignore or deny the political character of Jesus' ministry, they must assert that these officials misunderstood their prisoner – which flies in the face of the plain meaning of the narrative.

At the end of the arrest scene, Jesus accuses his adversaries of political impotence, since they are doing covertly what they did not dare to publicly (14:49). Nevertheless, this pressure from 'homeland security' is enough to cause all of Jesus' followers to flee the scene (14:50-52). This moment represents the collapse of the 'discipleship narrative' that has been central to Mark's gospel. It is important to acknowledge that as hard as Mark may be on the Judean authorities in this story, he is hardest on Jesus' own intimates. This is underlined by the tragic cameo of the disciple Peter's denial that Mark weaves into the trial narrative (14:54, 66-72).

Mark's trial narrative consists of two hearings, each of which presents a different charge against Jesus: blasphemy before the Sanhedrin (14:64), and sedition before Pilate (15:2). Both were capital offences in their respective juridical spheres. However, in Roman-occupied Palestine in the late Second Temple period it is unclear whether the Judean client government had the authority to execute the death penalty. While the majority of scholars contend that the Judean authorities did not have that power, the historian Josephus records an account of the stoning of James in *Antiquities* (XX, ix, 1), while Acts 6:8ff narrates the stoning of Stephen.

In either case, Mark's double trial construct must be explained. If the Sanhedrin did not need Roman approval to capitally punish heretics, then the fact that Mark included the hearing before Pilate means that he wished his readers to understand that Jesus was also wanted by the Romans on charges of sedition. If Roman approval was mandatory, on the other hand, we still have to explain why the Romans did the deed, rather than simply signing off on a Judean execution. This highlights the sole uncontested historical fact of the case: Pilate sentenced Jesus to crucifixion, which was a Roman penalty reserved exclusively for those convicted of insurrection. This can only mean that the Roman governor of Judea judged Jesus to be a substantial threat to imperial security.

Trying to avoid this obvious conclusion, the traditionally religious reading of Mark's trial has assumed that the Sanhedrin was 'using' Pilate for its own ends. As an historical assertion, this would have been impossible. Extrabiblical sources make it clear that of all the procurators stationed in Palestine during the Roman colonial period, Pontius Pilate (in Judea 25–36 CE) was one of the most ruthless. There is simply no historical evidence to suggest that Pilate could have been manipulated by the Judean leadership – much less by the 'crowds' (see 15:15). On the contrary, he was expert at playing the native aristocracy off against each other for his political ends.

Mark is not a modern journalist, however, but an ancient Christian polemicist. He took considerable literary license to draw characters in an unflattering light. If some aspects of his portraits seem historically implausible, they make perfect sense as a sort of ancient 'political cartoon', in which notorious figures are both unmistakably recognisable and clearly caricatured all at once.

An analysis of Mark's trial narrative reveals that he has constructed a careful parallelism between Jesus' two 'hearings'. Each consists of four aspects: trumped-up charges that are ironically fitting; a two-fold interrogation; the presiding judge 'consults' and convicts; and a final torture scene, in which Jesus is ridiculed, struck and spat upon. Moreover, the interrogations in the two trials are almost identical. Jesus either refuses to respond or returns the sarcasm of the prosecutor's 'naming' (see 14:61f and 15:2-5).

The function of this parallel composition was clearly not to implicate one party and exonerate the other. Quite the contrary: Mark wished to portray the Judean and Roman authorities as fully colluding in their railroading of Jesus, implying that both parties perceived him as a common enemy. And indeed, such cooperation between elites in a colonial situation is quite historically plausible, particularly in the politically volatile context of the high holy days, in which there was always the threat that popular movements for native sovereignty could get out of hand.

The aspects of Mark's account that are historically suspect, on the other hand, can be explained in terms of Mark's sharp literary polemic. There are strong elements of political parody in the gospel's grimly comic caricature of these proceedings. In this, Mark was following a long tradition in biblical literature, as Ze'ev Weisman has overviewed in his excellent study, *Political Satire in the Bible*: 'The role of the prophet as the assailer at the gate, who inveighs against manifestations of social and political corruption, frequently to the accompaniment of threats and even curses against the institutions and leaders of society, puts him in need of a polemic redolent with scorn, irony and wit.'

It is crucial for Christians to understand, however, that the critique of the Temple apparatus demonstrated by Mark's Jesus was social and economic, not religious. Mark portrays Jesus dramatically disrupting business as usual in the Temple courtyard (11:12-18), and lambasting the way in which poor widows were being exploited by wealthy scribes while standing in front of the Temple treasury (12:38–13:2). These episodes stand within the tradition of Jeremiah and Second Isaiah (both of whom Jesus quotes in 11:17). They represented Jesus' desire not to abolish the Temple cult, as Christian supercessionists imagine, but rather to challenge any institution that legitimated or perpetuated class oppression in Judea. Still, such a radical critique of the Temple was not likely to have been popular in a city largely economically dependent upon it, neither with the authorities who managed that apparatus nor with the local populace employed by it. Thus later some bystanders at the cross repeat the allegation (15:29).

Mark's Jesus makes no attempt to refute the charges (14:61) because he understands this is a political trial in which legal arguments are moot, and in which justice is subordinate to the need for conviction. In the end it comes down to the question of his self-identification.

Jesus demurs over the question of his 'Messianic' aspirations, instead invoking the witness of the 'Human One'

(14:62). This is an allusion to the biblical prophet Daniel's vision of the heavenly courtroom where true justice is vindicated (Daniel 7:9ff), and continues the apocalyptic thread that Mark has woven throughout the second half of his story (especially in chapter 13). According to Daniel, the heavenly Human One is the prosecutor of governmental 'beasts' who persecute the saints of God. And in Mark's gospel, Jesus-as-the-Human-One goes on the offensive against the local authorities (Mark 2:10, 28), the cosmic Powers (13:26), and finally here before the high court. It's this that pushes the court too far.

The high priest charges blasphemy (14:63f; see Leviticus 24:16). He then consults with the rest of the Sanhedrin to secure the conviction, and turns Jesus over to be tortured (Mark 14:65f. (It is worth noting that Mark states the abuses to Jesus in a few bare phrases, while Mel Gibson expands these into a tiresome and gruesome feature film!) His captors 'pommel' him (Greek *rhapismasin*, an allusion to Isaiah 50:6), and insist mockingly that he should 'prophesy'. This of course functions ironically, given that Mark understands Jesus to be following in the footsteps of the great prophet-martyrs – most recently John the Baptist (Mark 9:11-13).

From a literary point of view, we are in similar territory to Mark's earlier account of a party that Herod threw for the Galilean elite, in which the infamous 'dance of Salome' sealed the fate of John the Baptist (6:14-29). In that episode Mark is clearly parodying the decadent ways of the rich and powerful, complete with the absurd scenario of Herod allowing a dancing girl to determine the fate of an important political prisoner because of a drunken oath. Mark's trial scene is working in this same mode: as a polemic representing the point of view of the victim's followers.

Meanwhile, paralleling the first trial is the pathetic cameo of the wayward disciple Peter, narrated in 'split screen' fashion (14:66-72). Peter's denial of Jesus functions to contrast Jesus' simultaneous confession of the 'Human One' before the High Priest (14:62). Jesus is condemned while Peter goes free, playing out the ultimatum given by Jesus to his disciples at the midpoint of the story: 'Whosoever tries to save his life will lose it . . .' (8:34-38).

For Mark, Jesus' 'anticipation' of Peter's abandonment (14:27-31) or of his showdown with the nation's rulers (8:31-33; 9:31f; 10:32-34) is not a sign of divine omniscience, but of shrewd political realism. Those who speak truth to power must always face the consequences. And in the end, few indeed have the courage, character and conviction to walk that non-violent way.

The second part of Mark's political cartoon now turns to the other half of the colonial 'condominium': the Roman procurator. Pilate immediately (and correctly) identifies the issue as one of political authority in an occupied country: 'Are you King of the Judeans?' (15:2). This title was held by Roman client-rulers such as Herod, and from Pilate's perspective was a contemptuous reminder that the Jews were not truly sovereign in their own land. The true nationalist Messianic title would be 'King of Israel' (the designation used by the chief priests in their final taunt at the cross, 15:32).

In contrast to the traditional view of Pilate as an unwilling, equivocating participant in events beyond his control, Mark's account actually gives us a sketch of procuratorial pragmatism at work. He manages to send a prominent dissident to the gallows, while dividing the nationalist crowd against itself with the aid of the solicitous Judean clerical elite.

Initially Pilate, like the high priest, is unable to get Jesus to defend himself against the charges (15:3f). He is puzzled, thinking perhaps that this Galilean bumpkin doesn't understand the gravity of the situation (15:5). But then, in a shrewd public relations ploy aimed at playing the unruly crowd's patriotism off against itself, he decides to defuse the possibility of a popular uprising by granting a special, festival-specific amnesty (15:6). There was some historical precedent for such paternalistic gestures, though the evidence is scant. 'Barabbas' (whose name translates ironically as 'son of the father') is then introduced into the narrative as someone 'who had committed murder in the insurrection' (15:7). By this Mark likely means he was a Sicarii (Zealot) operative, insurgents who were known for political assassinations.

Mark's ensuing account means to dramatise the people's

fateful choice between two would-be 'revolutionaries' – the guerrilla terrorist and the non-violent prophet – who represented divergent paths to national liberation. The elements of the narrative that are most implausible historically – namely, the absurd fiction of the procurator 'consulting' the crowd (15:9, 12, 14), and the inconceivable spectacle of Jews calling for the crucifixion of one of their own (15:13f) – are fully consistent with a strategy of literary satire. I believe Mark's anti-imperial polemic is alluding here to the infamous Roman gladiator tradition, which to the Jewish mind would have represented the zenith of bloodthirsty pagan cynicism.

Against the backdrop of what we know of Roman gladiatorial games (see McManus and Weisman), Pilate's 'consultation' with (and possible taunting of) a Jewish crowd gathered outside the Roman *praetorium* concerning which prisoner should die becomes intelligible. So does Jesus' subsequent 'death march' to the 'place of the skull' (Mark 15:21f). This is Markan satire at its bitterest: the nationalist crowd, caught between the conflicting revolutionary claims of the urban guerrilla and the rural sign-prophet, gets co-opted by their imperial overlord into this most pagan ritual. Rome prevails, Judea remains under the boot, and Jesus becomes an imperial statistic.

Indeed, the fickle masses are central characters in the farce, and important to Mark's political message. In a matter of days the crowd has gone from 'hearing gladly' Jesus' criticisms of the priestly elite (12:37) to being manipulated by them to scream for his demise (15:11ff). They are truly 'sheep without a shepherd' (6:34), as Mark earlier put it, in the tradition of Ezekiel 34's fierce indictment of Israel's political leadership. The tragedy of course is that the people again succumb to the will of their political masters – who, according to Mark, actually fear them (see Mark 14:2)! This is why the shrieks of the crowd (15:13f) echo the wails of the demons in Mark (see 3:11; 5:5; 9:26) and the cries of the oppressed (see 9:24; 10:47f; 11:9).

The trial narrative concludes with Pilate's security forces making the parody complete. In the Roman military tradition of humiliating the defeated opponent, Jesus is disrobed and dressed up in a centurion's cloak and a 'laurel wreath' of thorns. These symbolise the very militarism and imperialism he has resisted with his life (15:16f). Once again he is mocked as 'king of the Judeans,' and 'worshipped' with insults, then disrobed again and led out to be crucified (15:18f). Needless to say, if Mark were trying to exonerate the Romans, this was hardly a flattering portrait!

Jesus is marched, in the grand tradition of Roman conquest, to the site of execution (15:20f). While the *via crucis* in Gibson's film is an agonising, interminable study in the worst kinds of pietistic Catholic *midrash*, Mark's version is spare and grim, needing no embellishment. This is because in his time, this public spectacle functioned to deter subversives and to aggrandise the Roman military presence. It inspired not beatific (voyeuristic? sadistic?) ecstasy in the beholder, as in the film, but sheer terror. So too the cross itself. To restive imperial subjects it conjured the fate awaiting those who dared challenge Caesar's sovereignty. To the 'civilised' it represented a form of punishment so inhumane that Cicero once urged that it be 'banished from the body and life of Roman citizens'. But to Mark's Jesus, it symbolised the cost of discipleship (Mark 8:34f) – and the end of the world (Mark 13:24-27; 15:33-38). That, however, is another story.

Mark's trial scene is indeed a caricature. It is not an anti-Semitic tract, however, but the work of a Jewish dissident who is deeply disillusioned with the leadership of his nation. At the time Mark wrote – which I take to be sometime during the war with Rome in 66–70 CE – the Jewish followers of Jesus were still experiencing prosecution by synagogue and/or Temple authorities (as suggested by e.g. Mark 10:29f and 13:9-11), and execution by Roman officials. So the gospel's 'victim/outsider' bias concerning Jesus' trial and death had stinging contemporary relevance. It both warned prospective disciples and comforted those already feeling the heat.

Mark's social criticism, though necessarily historically specific, is addressed to every culture and political formation. To limit it to late Second Temple Judaism is not only to miss his point badly, it is to perpetuate the murderous historical legacy of misunderstanding and oppression that has too often characterised the attitude of Gentile

Christians (and pseudo-Christians) toward the Jewish people. The opponents of Mark's Jesus were, to use apocalyptic language, 'powers', a rubric I believe embraces not only members of the Roman and Judean ruling classes then, but also imperial powers now – perhaps especially North America.

From the perspective of first-century Palestinian history, the cross was a Jewish symbol before it was a Christian one. Can the cross, which has for so long been a symbol of persecution for Jews on one hand, and a symbol of Docetic salvation for Christians on the other, be rehabilitated as a new symbol for the practice of non-violent resistance that might be embraced by both Jews and Christians?

The focus of Gibson's film is how Jesus died. The question of why Jesus was put to death, however, while of no interest to Gibson, is what Mark's gospel tried to address. The way Jesus died cannot, from Mark's perspective, be understood apart from the way he lived. His radical solidarity with the poor and outcast, his boundary-crossing and non-violent actions, his creative re-enactment of the prophetic legacy, and his criticism of those with wealth and privilege all got him into trouble with the authorities of his day. And those who carry on such practices today – from whatever religious and/or political affiliation – can reckon on receiving the same treatment, whether in East Timor or East Harlem, Colombia or Columbia Heights. *That* story would be a movie worth making.

## General Sources

1 John Dominic Crossan, 'Loosely Based on a True Story: The Passion of Jesus Christ in verbal and visual media', *Tikkun* online, 2004.
2 Alison Futrell, *Blood in the Arena: The spectacle of Roman power* (University of Texas, 1997).
3 Samuel N. Gordon, '*The Passion of the Christ* as seen through Jewish and Christian Eyes', occasional paper, Chicago Theological Seminary (Winter–Spring 2004).
4 Frederic Jameson, *The Political Unconscious: Narrative as a socially symbolic act* (Cornell University Press, 1981).
5 Barbara F. McManus, 'Arena: Gladiatorial Games' (The V-Roma Project, 1999).
6 Ched Myers, *Binding the Strong Man: A political reading of Mark's story of Jesus* (Orbis, 1988).

7 Willard M. Swartley (ed.), *Violence Renounced: René Girard, biblical studies and peacemaking* (Pandora Press/Herald Press, 2000).

8 Thomas Wiedemann, *Emperors and Gladiators* (Routledge, 1992).

9 Ze'ev Weisman, *Political Satire in the Bible* (Scholar's Press, Society for Biblical Literature, 1988).

# 7 Being delivered from Gibson's hell

**Anne Richards**

When we are immersed into the world of Mel Gibson's box office record-breaking film *The Passion of the Christ*, we can be in no doubt where we are. This is hell, and we are part of it. Hell is not some outer darkness in wait for the wicked after we die, but is present in the now of the film. In such a world, symbolic structures take on more significance: we are not viewing a linear narrative unfold in the course of watching the film. We are seeing the Gospel story coming apart through a series of symbolic layers. Consequently the sequence of the Passion narrative is interrupted by flashbacks to Jesus' childhood and ministry, which have a more naturalistic colour, tone and progression of dialogue. After Gethsemane, the descent into nightmare begins. Throughout, we have a hell's eye view of the development of events, until the perspective is dramatically reversed at Jesus' death and we suddenly have a 'God's eye view' of the whole drama, seen as from heaven, a heaven far away and from a great distance.

This hell world means that we view the film in an unusual way. Setting overtakes the 'story', and we are observing events which are being played out in a supernatural environment, not a 'realistic' one. In such a world, different rules apply: we are asked to consider what the world would look like if God's love and care for the creation were suddenly withdrawn, made absent, and the environment was under the control of infernal power. Some Jewish thinkers have examined the concept of the absence of God in respect of the hell of the Holocaust. Just such a sadistic and impotent world is represented here, as *this* Jew is tortured and murdered before our eyes.

So as the film opens, we see Jesus in Gethsemane (a weird, ghostly, supernatural world of full moon and blue darkness), tortured and tormented by the path he must take. And that path must entail separation from the Father; Jesus must himself enter hell and cleanse it. It is perhaps this that causes Jesus such mental torment. To do as the Father asks, he must enter that place where God is not, that place of alienation, forsakenness and despair. So the Devil, in the form of an androgynous being going to and fro upon the world and walking up and down in it, looks on the suffering Jesus and knows his pain. Indeed, the Devil seems almost a sympathetic character, locked into Jesus' consciousness, observing Jesus' mental suffering as he resists the Devil's kingdom. They do, after all, have history and the Devil knows very well who Jesus is.

When the Devil comments that the burden of salvation is too much for one man, it is as if the Devil already knows the extent of the suffering that Jesus must undergo to undo the evil world. The Devil's task in their relationship is to tempt Jesus from his obedience to God, as once was tried in the desert long ago, and in Gethsemane we see the serpent of disobedience issue from the Devil towards the suffering Jesus, offering, perhaps, a way out. But Jesus rises up and bruises the serpent's head. This is his spiritual decision, but he is also committed to the symbolic realm: he must be the second Adam who delivers us from the bonds of sin.

In the film, we learn, with Judas, all about this particular hell. Once he has taken the silver and betrayed Jesus, he is plunged into an intense mental torture which unites him irrevocably to the images of this hell-world. There is no way back, returning the silver will not stop the events which have been set in motion. Children turn into demons, 'satans', and pursue him, screaming that he is cursed. The hallucinatory world of Judas' pain is supported by the music of the film and the images of flame in torches and lamps. Beyond the city he finds himself cast out and broken next to the rotting, fly- and maggot-ridden corpse of the donkey that brought Jesus into Jerusalem. So it is he hangs himself with the rope bridle of Jesus' dead donkey and thus finds release in death from the Devil's own domain.

Gibson keeps up the infernal imagery throughout the

75

film. Barabbas is a grinning lunatic with a clouded eye like the child demons. The court of Herod is filled with manic fools and leering monsters. Herod himself is grotesque and uncomprehending, unable to get beyond the rottenness that attends him and ironically dismissing Jesus as 'crazy'. Within each crowd scene, people stand with ugly, twisted faces, leering and snarling, parodies of human beings. When we look at the film, we cannot forget these images as again the Devil stalks among the crowd, caressing its own parody of a child. Within such a twisted world, it is ironic, but perhaps no surprise that Jesus himself is accused of blasphemy: he heals the sick and casts out devils by means of devils. Why should he not? God is far away from the minds of all these people; the Devil's work is all around.

The characteristic of such a world is the evil that men (*sic*) do. As within a Bosch painting, Gibson requires us to endure, with Jesus, all the pains humans can devise. Jesus is flogged with instruments of torture, at first just threatening weapons on a table, but then taken up by men seized with the pleasure of sadistic power and we see the results of such instruments, tearing chunks of flesh away and spattering the assailants with blood. Such instruments of hell are not just for keeping the faithful from straying, but used to confirm that this *is* hell, where pain, humiliation and suffering are the conditions of existence.

When the Latin word *satis* is spoken, it means 'enough', but we perhaps also cannot help but hear another word of which it is the root. When will the thirst to hurt and humiliate be *satis*fied? What is the extent of such degradation? The answer is that in hell, the torment must go on forever. Jesus is not flogged to death: he gets both punishment and crucifixion. So it is that when the bloody pulp of Jesus' broken body is crowned with thorns, he is hailed as the 'wormy king', lord of this underworld, his flesh as good as carrion. Is it perhaps intended to be ironic, then, when the film lingers on the symbols of torture removed from Jesus' dead body? The crown of thorns, the nailsand the splinters of wood lay abandoned. But for centuries such objects have been revered as connectors to Jesus' physical body within the saving event, regarded as overwhelmingly holy and sacred.

Similarly, the hellish sense of nightmare is maintained during the crucifixion scene. The Devil accompanies Jesus on the road to Calvary. The unrepentant thief is a snarling maniac, himself horribly tortured as the crow pecks out his evil eye. Every fragment of the torture of Jesus as he is nailed to the cross is preserved, lest we slip into the typical sanitised view of our hymns and prayers, the non-existent death of the pretty jewelled necklace. In hell, Jesus' arm is dislocated from its socket with a sickening wrench. In hell, we hear the nails pierce skin, flesh and bone. In hell, Jesus is turned over so the nails can be bent over fast and his weight pulls him earthwards into his appalling agony. As Jesus dies, we hear his cry of alienation and loss, his wail of despair. Thus we might have imagined the cry of the damned.

In this hell world, human beings are trapped in a kind of inertia. Within the film, even energetic fight scenes are transmitted to us in slow motion, as though the protagonists were stuck in treacle. In a hell world, no one has enough energy to change it or to save others. In such a world the only energy is derived from greed, pride, ambition, jealousy, hatred. Sin has made the clockwork of the world run down, so that just existing is exhausting. So the disciples in Gethsemane sleep, the women who love Jesus watch hopeless and in tears, Pilate can do nothing to change the way the clockwork is running. Most pitiful perhaps is the scene where Mary attempts to mop up the blood after Jesus' flogging, but the fact of the blood and the torture that went on cannot be soaked up or cleaned away.

Within this world are a number of symbolic indicators of Jesus' purpose and ultimate triumph. In the first instance, we have to learn to see Jesus as one who rises up, where we could not possibly ever do so. This begins in Gethsemane, where Jesus rises from his prostrate agony and crushes the snake. Again, during his torture, where he has been beaten to the ground, he rises to his feet, to be greeted with the amazed comment 'it is not possible'. On the road to Calvary, he falls again and again, but each time rises up until with Simon of Cyrene's help he comes to the place of his execution and is there raised up again. *Ecce homo.* Behold the man.

Jesus then, is the one who by word and deed asks us to look away from our entrapment in earth and dust and look heavenward, be fully human, not crawling as the serpent, but free and upright as God intends for us. This comes across powerfully in the flashback to the woman taken in adultery, as she crawls towards Jesus' feet utterly debased and ruined by sin and by condemnation. Yet Jesus takes her hand and raises her up.

Similarly we are required to focus on Jesus' acts of cleansing. Water is the antithesis of the fires of hell. So we see Jesus washing his hands after work, washing the feet of the disciples, washing before the Last Supper. After Gethsemane, ordinary cleansing is increasingly denied. Pilate tries to wash his hands clean, the women try to clean the blood, Veronica's cup of water is dashed from her hands. What will wash this hellhole clean? The importance of water and Jesus as cleanser of human sin come together as Jesus, having absorbed all this hellfire, says 'I thirst.' From his dead body, water pours, sending the centurion to his knees. With Jesus' death, the rain comes, and all the filth is washed away.

A powerful theme of the film, and one supported by the viewing of the film itself, is *witness*. Jesus' eye (the other is smashed shut early on) is a constant element in the visual data of the film, as he searches out those who would hold his gaze. Jesus' eye confirms for people who they are by what they do. When he looks at them they know themselves: Judas the betrayer, Peter the denier, Mary the helpless, tortured mother, her fate inextricably bound to her son's pain (why does God do this to his handmaid?). Jesus looks too on those who hurt him, interrogate him, scream abuse at him. It is his eye we discern in the tomb. Who would he recognise in us? The believer? The sceptic? The bewildered? The indifferent? Gaze is about the only transaction which effects something in the film and so this undergirds our own position as witnesses, 'trapped' in the cinema, watching but powerless to act, to change anything, to alter the story or help Jesus bear his cross. The unrelenting witness means there is no place or opportunity to reject brutality, inhumanity, the misuse of power, the enjoyment of another's pain. This then, is hell, where the Devil holds our eyes open to see and know what we have done.

So who has sent Jesus to cleanse hell? It is clear that the Father has sent Jesus to do his will in both physical and supernatural worlds. Through the events at Calvary, we are seeing the harrowing of hell happen. The mission of Christ includes being sent to endure fear, abandonment, suffering, punishment and death. The mission of Christ therefore includes being sent to hell by these means to fetch out those imprisoned by sin. Indeed, the film begins with the words *by his wounds we are healed*. The Father's will is implacable. 'You would have no authority over me, except it were given you from above.'

Mere human politics could not make this happen. And this is not an outcome of the natural world, but the supernatural world. We are left in no doubt about this because of the storm and earthquake that breaks the Temple. These huge forces are beyond nature: Jesus is the ultimate exorcist whose love cleans out the Devil's world. Finally we see the Devil howling in emptiness, alone. Love's work is done. And is the Father some merciless God to sacrifice his Son in this appalling way? Surely, in that last perspective of the God's eye view of Calvary, we are meant to see the first drop of storm rain that falls as the overflowing grief of the suffering Father as the broken body, the body of his only Son, dies.

What is it then, that effects this exorcism? Again we can see this is another symbolic layer in the struggle with the Devil. Jesus is sent to cleanse, restore and heal, but this sending is characterised by the sense of Jesus as gift to us. We see Jesus giving. He gives his body and blood at the Last Supper. He gives his body and blood in the flogging and the crucifixion. He speaks words of intercession to the Father; he asks for forgiveness for those who hurt him. He gives his mother to his friend to be mother and son together. Finally he gives his life.

Perhaps the most important glimpse of this ultimate giving is made known to us through the healing of the servant's ear in the Garden. Jesus gives his healing to the man and restores his ear. The man is not just restored, however, he is clearly utterly changed: healing goes far beyond the mere return of flesh and blood and release from physical pain. Jesus' healing has the power to lift human beings out of the Devil's own world and to give them unlooked-for freedom and life. In the film, the servant is purely amazed by it, overwhelmed by God's selfless gift bestowed on him. What on earth is he going to do with such a gift?

So what does it mean for *us* to enter this hell world and watch Jesus brutally and sadistically beaten, humiliated and tortured? One of the things the film surely tells us is that what we see is the stuff of our worst nightmares. Deep in our hearts is the fear that we will suffer, not as Jesus suffered, but as Mary suffered. That our loved ones, our children, will be taken and abused, raped and murdered, will be hurt by illness, will enter a place of torment where we cannot hold them and comfort them but only look on and weep.

And beyond our personal nightmare is the knowledge that in places of our world right now, that hell is very real for millions of people. They die in war, they die of famine, they die of AIDS, their bodies are ruined by poverty and abused by the rich. Some of them lie in unmarked graves; their bodies will never be tended and buried. In their world, the Devil stalks all day looking upon them, and we do little or nothing, seized with inertia like the disciples. We say piously in our prayers, 'Deliver us from evil', but offer no thanks that Jesus has done just that, nor do we turn enough of our minds to those whose prayer is for a whole transformation of their world.

At the very end of the film, the grave clothes fall back and Christ rises again. He leaves the screen – to do what, to go where? The world of the film ends and our world resumes. Does that not place some responsibility on us? Will we meet this risen Christ and know ourselves in his gaze? If so, how will others know it? Will we talk piously among ourselves of finding faith strengthened, our love of the Lord renewed? Or will we take the life Christ bought for us from the Devil's kingdom and live it in justice and truth and praise and glory?

# 8 Embodying the cross in the church of the bloody useless

## Kevin Scully

Has the cross become a symbol without meaning in our society? This is a question that underlies a number of the essays in this book. It may seem absurd to those who call themselves Christians. Yet for many in the West the cross appears to have become an accessory. It is a thing to be looked at, displayed, without entering into a world requiring imaginative or intellectual engagement.

The cross, often bejewelled and glistening, can be seen hanging louchely between the uplifted breasts of the rich and famous. Or it is dazzlingly on show in gangsta bling. This gives out confused signals. Is the wearer making a public profession of faith? Or is the symbol of salvation sublimated to the self-promoting dazzle of material success?

The same might be said of the fashion, no doubt 'so last year already', of hanging a number of plastic moulded rosary beads around the neck. Cheap to buy, simple to wear. I encountered one young man in London who had four around his neck. I asked him if he knew what they were or what they meant. The answer was simple. 'They don't mean anything,' he told me. 'They're just cool.'

If the cross can be voided of religious content, what of the suffering of the one who hanged there? Is a graphic depiction of the violence of the Passion of Jesus made anodyne by the fashionista if the signpost itself has lost all meaning?

The reality of the experience of Jesus in his last hours, the recreation of human suffering and our capacity to be moved by it, has been a vital part of religious culture. So it is something of a surprise to find that people are, in fact, shocked by the implications of the cross. Making the leap of imagination can lead to the leap of faith. Or faith may urge a believer to move more deeply into the shocking reality of the Passion of Jesus.

The ability to shock, to see the familiar in new ways, can be a power for good. A priest in the east end of London is still spoken of because he had painted black the corpus on the crucifix outside the church he served. It is remembered for two reasons. First, the priest himself was black, working in what was then considered a white working-class area. Second, Christ had not been seen in this way before. This fractured a common understanding. The questioning of the traditional – to some – blue-eyed, blonde-haired Jesus addressed basic beliefs. If this popular reception of Jesus the man could be challenged, what of his Passion?

For generations a simple reading of Scripture was enough to get deeper into the last hours of Jesus. In the Catholic tradition the arrival of Palm Sunday brought with it the long, sometimes drawn out, reading of the Passion account of the synoptic gospel of the year – Matthew, Mark or Luke. In the days between the Latin Mass and the advent of liturgy in the vernacular there was a double whammy. The first reading, to be listened to standing, was in Latin, with a later translation to be received in a similar posture. And the trial would be lengthened without variation on Good Friday when the longer Passion narrative of John was read.

Over the years other ways have been used to enliven the Passion reading. There are dramatic renderings in which the range of parts is shared among members of the congregation. Movement has been used to enhance the sense of journey in the story. After all, a leaden reading of the events from the arrest in the Garden of Gethsemane to the laying of the body of Jesus in the tomb could actually have the opposite of the desired effect. Rather than an engagement with the brutality meted out on the Christ, there might be a numbing sensation undergirded by a moving desire for the turgid reading simply to be over.

Yet the imagination can provide one of the most immediate methods of 'making real' the Passion. This can be of enormous import to believers and explorers alike. It is a step on the way to embracing the incarnation. If God wholly took on human form, then humans can use their faculties to move deeper into understanding the path that led from celebration to Christ's desolate end, hanging on a cross outside the city walls of Jerusalem.

There is ample precedent for this. A walk around any major art gallery in Western or Eastern Europe will provide numerous religious images. The events of the Passion, taking in the memorial meal that the church terms the Last Supper, the agonised praying of Jesus in the Garden, his betrayal to the armed mob with a kiss from Judas, his trials, his maltreatment at the hand of soldiers and the torturous walk up to Golgotha, are vividly displayed. Much of the source of this art comes directly from Scripture. The works are attempts to broaden the perspective of that caught in the words of the gospels.

Such a combination of moving encounters is also enshrined in the Stations of the Cross to be found in many churches. The scenes, scriptural or apocryphal, which make up the traditional fourteen stations, capture and trigger many emotions. Fingers point to accuse. Soldiers taunt and beat the prisoner. Shouting envelops the procession of the man condemned to the place of execution. Women meet him on the way. He is stripped of his clothes. Nails are driven into his hands. He dies. His body is laid in a tomb.

With the imagination – one of the gifts of God in creation – we can enhance these scenes in our mind's eye. We can discover afresh the reality in what is presented through our senses. We are able to turn what we see into something greater than the visual. We can hear, touch, smell and taste. Our bodies can bring us closer to the suffering of the incarnate God. As he shared our senses, we can use our minds to come closer to God. And we are able to place ourselves in the pictures as a participant or witness.

The film *The Passion of the Christ* can be seen as part of this tradition. Taking the stories and enhancing the material with the techniques of cinema, we can see more deeply, hear raucously and be moved for good or ill. We can sympathise. Or we can be revolted. We can be inspired. Or we can be horrified. For many Mel Gibson's film has itself become part of what another famous movie entitled *The Greatest Story Ever Told*.

This is available to anyone, regardless of faith. But for those who make up the community of believers, the church, it is a devotional path to deepen the apparent. It often has surprising results. A place of worship that is familiar to many becomes new when aspects of it are made the focus of attention. This can happen anywhere and take many forms. Imaginative leaps can be both comforting and disturbing. What follows is just one example, from the church of St Matthew, Bethnal Green, in the east end of London.

In the centre of a relatively neglected churchyard lies the church building. The exterior retains mostly the lines envisaged by George Dance the Younger. But the interior is surprising, thanks to an imaginative refurbishment by Antony Lewis after damage caused by an incendiary bomb dropped during the Second World War. A wide, open space, with windows on two levels, the upper ones being for the removed galleries. The internal surfaces boast a number of original art works which are integral to the building.

Among these is a stunning set of stations by Don Potter. These scenes follow both the traditional number of four-teen stations and customary pattern of starting at the northeast corner of the church, crossing over the west wall and up to the front of the church again on the south side. After the first arched window to the right as one stands at the front door is the twelfth station. It boasts many unique qualities when compared to its fellows. The first is simple. It is larger than the rest. The other stations, some made in pieces in the wood-fired kilns which differentiated the colours, are effectively unified tableaux.

In the twelfth station the space which separates partici-pants is actually the fabric of the wall. Two of the three figures stand, individuals apart yet connected to each other by the unifying intermediate *mise en scene* of the rood of the Calvary hill. The artist has introduced an arresting facet to the scene with its central cross. In the stations previous to this one it has been a sombre hue, changing subtly because of the making process. In the twelfth station it has become piecework of golden mosaic. Hundreds of small glistening stones combine to create the lifeless arboreal limbs which have transmuted into the tree of life. Pinioned to this glowing instrument of death is the body of Jesus.

The scene has an ambivalent quality: the torso of Jesus looks strong but the arms are pinned. The head droops along his right arm. The arms, and the crossbar of the crucifix which gleams behind it, form a canopy. It is hard to know whether Potter is portraying Jesus as weak and still alive or as already dead. On either side of the golden mosaic cross stand the mother of Jesus and the beloved apostle, John.

To the left is Mary. She cannot or does not raise her eyes to the spectacle of her dying son. Many have meditated upon this scene since its installation in 1961. There is much to ponder: the tortured son hanging in front of the tortured woman; the aging young girl who accepted the challenge of God to conceive miraculously and bear a son. This boy, as she was told by the angelic visitor, would be 'great and will be called the Son of the Most High, and the Lord God will give to him the throne of his ancestor David' (Luke 1:32).

It is almost inevitable that viewing the scene of the crucifixion gives pause to the apparent irony of this. The faithful declare their allegiance to a king whose throne is an instrument of abuse. They see his rule, a never-ending kingdom according to the angel Gabriel, for what it is: pinioned by the earthly elements and nailed down.

In the scene that Don Potter has made, Mary is there, but seemingly disconnected. She is distracted, involved in her own grief. John is not much different. He too looks to the earth but there is a wonderful element in his stance. It is an unusual and subverting element to the traditional rendering of the scene. While John is looking away from the suffering servant on the cross, his right arm is extended and his hand touches the gold of the crucifix.

What can be read from this contact? Suppose that the man whose touch healed so many in the accounts of his life has given up the ghost. John has then absorbed a lifegiving and caring commission from his teacher. In the gospel which bears his name John is given the care of Jesus' mother. 'When Jesus saw his mother and the disciple whom he loved standing beside her, he said to his mother, "Woman, here is your son." Then he said to the disciple, "Here is your mother." And from that hour the disciple took her into his own home' (John 19:26-27).

Even in the face of death Jesus had the power to change lives. The responsibility of care for his mother, an inversion of the parental concern, is given to someone else. This incident is often seen in the context of its emotion: a man who, in the midst of his pain, near to death, shows his love by ensuring the ongoing welfare of the mother he loved. And yet the scene has both limiting and empowering corollaries.

The first is simple. Mary is enshrined as chosen. God sent his angel to her to tell her of her undeserved election.[1] ' "Greetings, favoured one! The Lord is with you." But she was much perplexed by his words and pondered what sort of greeting this might be' (Luke 1:28-29). The words from the cross echo the status of her special qualities. To that end she is given first to be the bearer of God, then is given by God made man into the care of his followers. It is of no surprise that Mary holds a special place in the life of the church. It is the very ordinariness of her, devoid of the accretions of Immaculate Conception and the like, which commends her. What is intriguing is how much energy is expended challenging that view.

Don Potter catches the challenge of this exchange. John's hand is touching the cross. He, as the church has been, is sent out. While he is there in the twelfth station of the cross, he has been told by the Christ to leave. He has been given a task. This is another version of the many commissions that Jesus gives those who would follow him. The call of conversion is more than prayerful meditation on the teachings and events of the life of Jesus. He repeatedly tells his followers to take on tasks: to spread the good news, to do as the good Samaritan, to love enemies, to question claims of earned righteousness over the grace of God. This they have attempted, and still try, to do with varying degrees of success

Why is it, then, that this touching of the cross is turned by some in the church to a dead centre from which only paralysis can flow? Where are *we* to start? John's commission was immediate. The person he had to care for was next to the cross where he himself was standing. Standing at the foot of the rood, we are wondering at the extent of the challenges which the world presents. What can we do in the face of such forces which deprive the world of justice?

To some the church is becoming turned in on itself. Critics say that church members seem more interested in their own issues, or recruiting spiritual clones, than responding to the many issues facing humanity. Such efforts leave little enthusiasm for matters beyond the confining cell of right-minded fellow travellers. This creeping lassitude is both dangerous and subversive to the profession of the Christian faith. Yet it is also sometimes a necessary reality check for those who imagine that their faith, combined with their good works, will change the course of human events. The faith calls us to try. In some cases, we may succeed. But Jesus did offer warnings about the enormity of the task when he urged that it should be done: 'For you always have the poor with you, and you can show kindness to them whenever you wish' (Mark 14:7).

There are times when we are at risk of becoming the church of the bloody useless. Worries about our own survival, distress and argument over supposed doctrinal verities, obsession about finances, can become the very stuff of life. The Church of England, for some still the heart of the nation's spiritual life, is at risk of becoming merely the church accountant here on earth. There are repeated crises of fiscal and personnel management. Initiative follows initiative with one thinly veiled message: more people and more money are needed for survival. Some of its members shriek at others for breaches of claimed, supposed or even imagined, purity.

Arguments about sexuality, money and internal politics make good copy for those reporters who can be bothered with the institution. For those outside the sub-culture of media reductionism the church and thereby the Christian way are, not surprisingly, a turn off. They decide them to be irrelevant to their personal needs, if not to the society in which they are based. This is a twist on the maxim of

Groucho Marx, 'I don't want to belong to any club that will accept me as a member.' Instead, it becomes who wants to join an organisation like the church when it is saying: 'because you are not a hand you do not belong to the body, at least not the body of which I am a member. So I am not going to share my bread, especially not with the likes of you'?

The church is at risk of losing that empowering touch shown by John's hand to the cross. It needs to keep contact with the wood of the cross while acknowledging the issues it faces. The church should be one organisation that transcends the borders of wealth and self-interest. If we use Paul's metaphor of the body, then the strong, the comfortable and wealthy should be supporting those who are weak, unsettled and poor. This is a task of imaginative action. Especially where its own members are trying to carry out the dual tasks of building a faithful community which connects to its surroundings. If it does not it becomes the grave heart that St Matthew's, Bethnal Green is at risk of being: listed, surprising, beautiful, but bloody useless.

## Notes

1 For some this is shocking. But it should not be. The story of Mary is consistent with others in Scripture. Those who are beloved of God do not, on the whole, do anything to deserve their special status. This is true of Adam, Noah and Abraham who received the blessing of God. It is this blessing that led to their pre-eminence. They did nothing to earn it. As it is said of Noah, he simply 'found favour in the sight of the Lord' (Genesis 6:8). What follows in the stories of each is the awareness of the blessing and, in some cases, where they have fallen short of it.

# 9 Atonement, violence and modern imperial order

## Michael Northcott

The war in Iraq, which began in 2003 and at the time of writing has seen approximately 100,000 lives lost in violence[1] (in addition to the looting and burning of hospitals and schools, the widespread destruction of water and electricity supplies, and the complete dissolution of the public services, police and army of the most advanced state in the Middle East), was initiated by the leader of the most powerful nation on earth, George W. Bush. Like the Emperor Constantine in the third century of the Christian era, Bush is a convert to Christianity, and when he announced the 'war on terror' against those who had attacked America in 2001 he spoke of a 'crusade' against 'evil-doers'.

There was no connection between Iraq and the attack on America but this did not stop Bush launching his war, nor Muslims throughout the world interpreting air strikes on civilian areas, the use of cluster bombs on villages and suburbs, the sacking of Baghdad, and the later destruction of Fallujah, as a punitive enterprise of the Christian West against Muslims. The widely documented use of torture by American and British forces in their subsequent treatment of Iraqi prisoners, and the many deaths in custody of prisoners of war, seemed to be part of a larger pattern in which America and Britain had abandoned the Geneva Conventions, which are internationally agreed codifications of Christian just war principles designed to restrain the evils of war, in favour of a mode of warfare as retribution and revenge. Any who would doubt this might recall the chilling words of Donald Rumsfeld, the American Defence Secretary, who announced during the first post-2001 punitive war in Afghanistan that it would be appropriate for enemy combatants to be summarily executed.[2]

This is not the first time Britain and America have invaded and subdued Muslim lands. Ever since the tenth and eleventh centuries, and in particular the enterprises of King Richard the 'Lionheart' who unilaterally – that is without the support of the French – led his crusaders to a battle with Saladin for Jerusalem which ended in a violent subduing and occupation of that city, Muslims have perceived their relation to the Christian West through the lens of the crusade. But whence does the language of the crusade come within the Christian tradition?

For many years as a child I attended an organisation which calls itself the Crusaders. It had a logo which clearly referred back to the enterprise of the first Crusaders and, as well as attending weekly Crusader classes where we certainly did sing the hymn 'Onward Christian Soldiers' on occasion, I also went to Crusader Camps in the summer. Our round bell tents in fields, and camp kitchens and fires, were even a little reminiscent of the camps of the Crusaders of old as they amassed in the desert to fight with the Muslim hordes.

The Crusaders is a Christian evangelical youth movement whose central tenet of faith, like most modern Protestant evangelical denominations and para-church groups, emanates from the innovations of the Reformers in atonement theology. John Calvin and Martin Luther saw the death of Jesus Christ on the cross as the violent punishment which God exacted from his Son in payment of the penalty which human sin required a righteous God to impose upon the human race.[3] We were taught as Crusaders that it was only because Christ had paid this penalty and satisfied the wrathful judgement of God the Father that we were saved. The cross of Christ was presented to us in this way as the first Crusade, and as the only possible way in which God could have redeemed the human condition.

For most of Christian history the Church has not made the theology of the atonement an article of credal faith. Neither the Apostles' Creed nor the Nicene Creed identify any one of the events of Christ's birth to a virgin, his life, death, resurrection and ascension, or his gifting of the Spirit, as *the* saving event.[4] Rather they invite us to confess and celebrate all these events as part of a larger narrative in which God showed Godself to redeem the fallen world by becoming one with sinful human flesh, while also remaining 'one, of one substance, with the Father'.

Yet when I went to university I found that the evangelical Christian Union (CU) that I attended required me to sign a different credal statement in which I had to affirm that the one atoning and sacrificial death of Jesus was the redeeming punishment for my sins and therefore the key to Christian salvation. I attended CU meetings, played the guitar at Christian missions, I went out with (and then married) a CU girl, but I never signed the card. I did not believe then, and do not now, that this was a truthful account of a Christian understanding of salvation.

Religion is at its heart about mimesis, as anthropologists are fond of pointing out. It is about acting out, copying, repeating, through ritual, the events which God (or the gods) are said to have marked out as the means by which a people have become God's people. If the central event of the Christian story of divine salvation is about violent retribution, then it would be unsurprising if over their history Christians had not begun to copy and act out this violent retribution in their relations with people of other faiths, and in their punishment of criminals and heretics. And of course it was precisely this mimesis of violence and punishment which marred the Christian era from at least the twelfth century onwards.

The crucial event in this turn in atonement theology and practice was the conversion of Constantine, and ultimately the turn of Christianity into the official religion of the Roman Empire. Until this event Christians had been a persecuted minority who were frequently martyred for their faith. They gave an account of their faith which did not allow them the option of the use of violence; according to Hippolytus even where members of the army became Christians they were to resist military authority where it required them to kill or to be trained in killing.[5]

But the turn of Christianity into an imperial religion fostered an account of a 'righteous empire' from Eusebius onwards and it was only a century later that Augustine of Hippo formulated the first Christian account of justified war. These dramatic shifts in the social position of the church, and in Christian attitudes to imperial power and violence, inevitably impacted on Christian representations of the salvation story, as can clearly be seen in Christian art. In the first four centuries the cross is rarely found as an image in Christian places of worship or in Christian mosaics and paintings. Instead we find the *Chiro* – a combination of the first two letters of the Greek word Christ – as the most common symbol of Christian belief, along with the fish, the good shepherd and one or two other recurring images.[6]

After the turn of Christianity into an imperial cult, however, the cross begins to appear more frequently in Christian imagery and symbolism. Early cross images depict a clothed and crowned Christ the King whose arms are outstretched on the cross but who is in the form of the resurrected and ascended heavenly Lord who has resumed his seat in heaven on the right hand of God. Moreover, by the Middle Ages artists begin to depict Christ on the cross as a bleeding, dying, tortured and naked body.[7]

In the Middle Ages there also arose a new and influential teaching about the atonement, first put forward by Anselm of Canterbury in his *Cur Deus Homo* (Why God Became a Man) where he argued that the death of Christ was a transaction between God and God's Son in which the obedience of the Son unto death was the only way in which God's righteousness could be satisfied and the wrongs of sin righted. The cultural context for Anselm's writing was the new form of hierarchical feudalism and seignorage which had overtaken the formerly relatively non-hierarchical Anglo-Saxons and Celts of the British Isles after the Norman conquest. And his theological innovation was also, as Daniel Bell argues, a reflection of the penitential practices of the medieval church.[8]

Anselm's theological innovation placed the concept of divine satisfaction close to the heart of the Western Christian understanding of salvation history, but it was not until the Reformers that the idea that this satisfaction was quite literally *penal* emerged. It was Calvin who first claimed that Christ received 'God's vengeance' on the cross, in order 'to appease his wrath and satisfy his just judgement'.[9] It was this penal theory which, in the Westminster Confession, and in Cranmer's Articles of Religion, was given credal form by the Reformers in England. At the time of Anselm's innovation the Church had already begun to practise violence against heretics, invented the notorious Inquisition to deal with Catalan heretics, and even adopted a standing papal army, remnants of which can still be seen in the fortified citadel of the Vatican to this day, though it was not until the Reformation itself that the true potential of this doctrine to legitimate violence was fully realised.

The penal substitution theory of the atonement has come in for much criticism in recent times, not least from feminist and black theologians, precisely because of its contextual links with Christian and European imperialism, with the violence of medieval and Reformed Christendom, colonialism and slavery, and thence with racism and patriarchy. The lonely male judge of feudal theology has acted since the late Middle Ages as a legitimator of wars of conquest, of patriarchy, and of violent forms of punishment, including torture and execution. But not only was this penal atonement theology problematic in its social consequences, it was also unfaithful to traditional Christian belief and practice. It replaced the narrative of salvation which had served for the first 1000 years of Christian history and which was concerned with the totality of the biblical narration of creation and fall, incarnation, crucifixion and resurrection, the gift of the Spirit and the calling of the Saints: *altogether* these events constituted Christian salvation.

The new penal theory was also a departure from the traditional teaching of the Apostles and the Fathers about what actually happened in and around the crucifixion of Christ. As the Swedish theologian Gustav Aulén argued in his classic essay *Christus Victor* the cross was the place where Christ *triumphed* over the fallen powers – the Temple authorities, the Roman imperial power, the rule of the mob – which Christ had challenged in his earthly ministry.[10] These fallen powers thought they had killed the Lord of Glory but instead, as St Paul puts it, he 'led captivity captive' (Ephesians 4:8) on his way from the cross to the resurrection. For the early Christians it was the *resurrection* and not the crucifixion which was the determinative, the truly saving event, for, as St Paul says 'if Christ has not been raised, your faith is futile' (1 Corinthians 15:17). It is only in the light of the resurrection that the sacrifice of the life of Christ can be seen as a sacrifice which has any meaning at all.

It is not that it was *not* a sacrifice but to argue that it was a sacrifice required by God without which God could not have saved the human race – to argue this is to misconstrue the true wonder and glory of our Easter faith.[11] Sacrifice it surely was, but the question for the first theologians was who required this sacrifice, and to whom, if it was a ransom, was the ransom paid. The answers to these questions were relatively straightforward. The sacrifice was required by those who imposed it as a punishment – the Jewish Temple authorities, the Roman imperial representative in Judea, and the mob. And if it was a ransom it was paid not to God but to the Devil and to the fallen powers through which the Devil had usurped the reign of God on earth since the Fall.

As Stuart Murray points out earlier in this volume, these answers became less acceptable once the Roman Empire had become putatively Christian, and the powers that claimed still to rule the earth sought partnership with the bishops and priests of the new people of God. So it was that in the fourth century Gregory of Nyssa changed the earlier account of the ransom paid to the Devil into a story where the Devil is *deceived* by the bait of Jesus on the cross and is thereby captured and defeated, a version of the story which, as McClendon suggests, could easily serve as legitimation of the kinds of things a 'righteous empire' might seek to do to maintain its rule.[12]

The leaders of the United States of America since 2001 have openly embraced the language of righteous empire. George W. Bush in particular has frequently linked the right of America to impose its will on distant nations with his self-understanding as a Christian president and leader of a nation that is righteous in its values and forms of life.

And the United States can lay a claim to being the most actively Christian nation in the West – 40 per cent of its citizens claim not just to be Christian but evangelical Christians and to attend church weekly. But the United States is also the most violent of all the democracies which have been birthed since the Enlightenment. And the violence is not just directed towards its enemies.

A postgraduate student of mine told me that he returned to the US after the terrible events of 11 September 2001 and found that all his friends in Seattle, including a number of evangelical Christians, now carried guns whenever they went on public transport, and kept them in their houses. The United States punishes by execution more than any other Western nation, and Texas more than any other state, and since 1945 the United States has bombed or invaded forty-nine countries. Violence – Rambo style, Clint Eastwood style – is the American way, it is at the heart of America's story about itself.[13]

The problem for us as Christians is that violence is also at the heart of American evangelical Christianity. The Southern states, which do the most executing, are the most conservative and evangelical states. The very same states which teach the doctrine of creation alongside evolution in their public schools are those states who execute the largest number of criminals. If religion is mimesis, and evangelical conservative Christians are committed to a view of their salvation which is intrinsically violent – which sets the necessity of violent punishment in the heart of the being of God, which even sets God as wrathful Father against God as Son on the Cross – then the violence of America is Christian violence.

Now of course by no means all evangelicals are committed to the violent course that the American judicial system, American gun ownership, and American foreign policy involves. Progressive evangelicals such as Jim Wallis and Ron Sider were prominent in opposing the 2003 invasion of Iraq and in critiquing the use of America's military power to exact retribution from Muslim nations for the attack on America in 2001. And it is at least as much the technological prowess and political power of the military industrial complex in and beyond America since the end of the

95

Second World War which is responsible for the cult of violence. But there clearly is a problem about Christianity, atonement and violence that we do well to understand. Jesus charges the disciples at his final resurrection appearance in the gospel of Luke to witness to a Gospel of repentance and forgiveness of sins to all the nations.

This is the Christian witness; this is what resurrection means – not war or violent punishment, but mercy and forgiveness. Spreading this message brought the first Christians into conflict with the governing powers, as it does still today in places such as China and Sudan, and, in the context of the emergence again of the idea of America as a righteous empire, in America itself, and in countries such as Britain who uncritically serve and support this new imperialism. But when such conflict arises the Christian witness of resistance will be non-violent if Christians truly remain faithful to the victory over sin and evil which was won with the resurrection of Jesus Christ from death on the cross.

Their proclamation of this victory involved the first Christians in a clear conflict with the violence and wealth of the Roman Empire. The gospels clearly and unambiguously depict Jesus as a non-violent teacher. He teaches non-violence and he acts out non-violence, peaceableness, in his person and in the way of the cross. Living out the way of non-violence in a violent imperial culture means that Christ was killed even though he was innocent. And it is precisely as the *innocent* victim that Christ's death opposes the violence of those who oppose the reign of God. As J. Denny Weaver puts it 'his death unmasks the powers of evil, and renders empty their claim that peace and order are founded on violence.'[14] The reign of God is not founded on violence because God is from eternity a non-violent God. Violence is a consequence of the Fall of humanity – it plays no part in God's way with God's world.

The option of non-violence for the Church is not then simply an option – it is a requirement if Christians believe that God truly reigns, is truly victorious, in the resurrection of Jesus Christ. As Weaver says: 'those who believe in the Resurrection perceive the true nature of power in the universe. Resurrection means that appearances can be deceiving. Regardless of what appears to be the case from an earth-bound perspective' – such as the seeming triumph of tyranny and war in human history since the first century – 'the Resurrection demonstrates the power of God's rule over all evil.'[15]

This is the Easter faith – it commits Christians not to the necessity but to the ultimate and divine impossibility of violence as a means to redeeming the human condition. Those Christians who claim that only through war can peace be attained are committed to another view of the atonement, a view which has to dismiss the non-violent teaching of the Jesus of the gospels as a perfectionist ethic, only good for monks, sectarians and pacifists who care not for the fate of the innocent, who would not resist tyranny. But it would be completely wrong to understand the Jesus of the gospels as one who commends non-resistance to evil.[16] It was Christ's resistance to evil – for example when he challenged the authority of the Temple religion over the Jewish people by offering to forgive the sins of the paralytic man – which entailed his following the way of the cross, and it is in Christ as risen victor that Christians understand that evil *is* overcome, overthrown, not by violence but by the reign of a non-violent God.[17]

So although truth and effectiveness are by no means the same thing, as John Howard Yoder often reminded us,[18] it is notable that in the last thirty years those 'regime changes' which have seen the subsequent establishment of relatively peaceable and democratic societies include the overthrow of Marcos by 'people power' in the Philippines, the overthrow of communism in Eastern Europe in the 'velvet revolution' and the end of the apartheid regime in South Africa. By contrast Iraq and Afghanistan look like remaining quagmires of civil war and strife for many years to come.

## Notes

1 Les Roberts, Riyadh Lafta, Richard Garfield, Jamal Khudhairi and Gilbert Burnham, 'Mortality Before and After the 2003 Invasion of Iraq: Cluster sample survey', *The Lancet* Vol. 364 (27 October 2004), p.1834.

2 As Oliver O'Donovan suggests, it is a measure of the influence of Christendom that Rumsfeld's suggestion was met with a 'widespread shudder of dismay' in Europe: Oliver O'Donovan, *The Just War Revisited* (Cambridge University Press, 2004), p.37.

3 James McClendon gives a fine summary of the Reformed innovation in his *Doctrine: Systematic theology Vol. II* (Abingdon Press, 1994), p.206.

4 Nicholas Lash, *Believing Three Ways in One God* (SCM Press, 1992), p.59.

5 Hippolytus, *Apostolic Tradition*, 2.16.

6 See further Patrick Sherry, *Images of Redemption: Art, literature and salvation* (T&T Clark, 2003).

7 I owe this observation to Rita Nakashima Brock in her paper 'The Cross and Communities of Life Restored' delivered at the 2003 meeting of the Society for the Study of Theology in Newcastle University.

8 Daniel Bell, 'Deliberating: Justice and liberation', in Stanley Hauerwas and Sam Wells (eds), *The Blackwell Companion to Christian Ethics* (Blackwell, 2003), pp.182-95.

9 Calvin, *Institutes* II, 16, 10 f. cited McClendon, *Doctrine*, p.206.

10 Gustav Aulén, *Christus Victor: An historical study of the three main types of the idea of atonement* (Macmillan, USA, 1969).

11 René Girard argues that Christ's death is nowhere interpreted as a sacrifice in the gospels or in the Epistle to the Hebrews in his *Things Hidden Since the Foundation of the World*, trans. Stephen Bann and Michael Metteer (Stanford University Press, 1987), pp.180ff. But Stanley Hauerwas argues that Christ's death was a 'sacrifice to end sacrifice' and John Milbank suggests that it was 'an effective sacrifice that overcame sacrifice': Stanley Hauerwas, 'Interview with Jim Wallis', *SojoNet*, November 8, 2001 and John Milbank, *Being Reconciled: Ontology and pardon* (Routledge, 2003), p.100.

12 McClendon, *Doctrine*, p.202. This is the version of the atonement that C. S. Lewis renders in his *The Lion, the Witch and the Wardrobe* (Collins, 1965). The witch is deceived by the death of the lion which satisfies the 'deep magic from before the dawn of time'.

13 See further Michael Northcott, *An Angel Directs the Storm: Apocalyptic religion and American empire* (I. B. Tauris, 2004).

14 J. Denny Weaver, *The Nonviolent Atonement* (Eerdmans, 2001), p.48. See also the extended argument in Weaver's contribution to this volume.

15 Weaver again.

16 At this point I cannot go along with John Howard Yoder in his account of non-resistance in *The Politics of Jesus: Vicit Agnus Noster* (Eerdmans, 1972). Walter Wink's account of non-violent resistance is closer to the *Christus Victor* theme: see his *Engaging the Powers: Discernment and resistance in a world of domination* (Fortress Press, 1992).

17 See further Stanley Hauerwas, 'Out of the Silence' in *First Things* (January/February 2002) at http://www.bigbrother.net/~mugwump/Hauerwas/

18 John Howard Yoder, *The Politics of Jesus* (Eerdmans, 1972).

# 10  The cross, salvation and the politics of satire

**Simon Barrow**

The location was a church hall in central London. The meeting was about to start. People of many faiths and none were present. The subject under discussion was the abuse of human rights and what, in practical terms, we could do about it. A hand went up somewhere near the back of the room. It was Albert, someone I knew well and valued. He was a great campaigner for justice, a pacifist and a humanist. But he had an objection.

'Before we begin', said Albert, 'could I record a protest that we are meeting in a room that displays a hideous image of an act of brutality and torture which the people who put it there think is edifying. I don't; I think it's disgusting and I'd prefer that it was removed.' There were puzzled looks. Instantly, I knew what he was talking about. For on the wall in front of us was a very large crucifix.

When the Christians in the room realised what was up, they groaned. Here was Albert trying to point-score against religion again, they sighed. Except he wasn't. He was quite serious and very offended. But his remark was dismissed with no further thought; a quick vote (in which Christians were in a majority, and thus able to sweep aside the objection), and the meeting went on as if nothing had happened.

I was troubled by this little episode, and it has stayed with me for the ensuing twenty-five or more years. The difficulty, you see, is that Albert was right about the cross and the Christians were wrong. He recognised it as a symbol of horror that ought to revolt any sensitive person. In this sense he, an atheist, was in a far better position to understand its true significance than many multitudes of believers who can deploy all kinds of theological rationales, as and when required, but show little sign of ever having been confronted with the true offensiveness of 'Christ crucified'.

Yet Christ crucified is exactly what the Gospel (good news, allegedly) is about. Crucified *and risen*, for sure. But, understood in the way the New Testament presents it, rather than in the way that it has been cheapened and sentimentalised by Christian piety, the impact of the resurrection is not to remove the offence, but to make it even more inexplicable and awful.[1] If God can raise Jesus, why cannot God rescue Jesus, the Innocent One, from unwarranted torture and death? To theorise that God *wants* it this way doesn't solve the problem, either. It makes God into an assassin.

St Paul recognised the problem instantly. He describes the Gospel of God in Christ, hanging helpless on a tree, as 'foolishness to the Greeks' (the wise sophisticates) and 'a stumbling block to the Jews' (the pious, religious people), because the message that God is to be found, not in glory and power, but in agony and powerlessness, offends against everything within us. It makes a nonsense of God, who is supposed to be all-powerful, and it ridicules suffering by saying that God participates in it rather than abolishing it.[2]

The attempt to 'make sense' of this just offends further against reason and humanity. And if that wasn't bad enough, Paul then goes on to make things much worse by claiming that 'Christ crucified' is the power of God to those who recognise God's salvation in it, and only a problem for those who are 'being lost'. This is one of the accusations I confidently predict will be levelled against this book. 'You people only have a difficulty with penal substitutionary atonement – the idea that God requires the death of his innocent Son in order to appease his wrath and be in a position to forgive sinners – because you are faithless. If not, you'd have no problem.'

But this misunderstands what is at stake entirely. The doctrine of penal substitution had not even been conceived when Paul was writing his letters to the various Christian communities he was in contact with. So the 'offence' and 'stumbling block' he describes is not to do with this theory.

In fact, in his writings, St Paul offers a number of images of what God is up to in the death of Jesus, and none of them is forensic, juridical and feudal in the way that subsequent Christian doctrinal formulation was. The difficulty for many today is not with the biblical testimony, but with the fact that this testimony has been squashed and smoothed out into a singular theory which some loud and influential people wish to require everyone to accept as *the* understanding of the Gospel. But we won't, because we think it profoundly distorts and compromises the Christian message and the way people receive it.

You see 'penal substitution' isn't foolishness to narrow rationalists, it's perfect sense. It fits exactly with how they see the world. This is because what passes for Christian fundamentalism is not a biblical creed, but a creed which fits biblical texts into a pre-ordained intellectual framework that actually works against many of them. What the 'one, literal meaning' advocates cannot get their heads around is that the Bible is rarely singular in what it says, and sometimes far from literal in its form or function. If it looks uniform, this is because we have not examined the text adequately. We have started instead with some idea that God, surely, would offer us not something 'open to interpretation' but something fixed and certain.

But this is not what God has done, because God is not like our human ideas about what a god 'should' be like. God, so the gospels tell us (all four of them, in different and not always even ways) is actually exposited by Jesus in his life, death and resurrection. This is what God is 'like'. That is where Paul starts too. In other words, God comes to us not as a knock down theory, an infallible book, an unassailable proposition or a self-evident 'answer'. Rather, God comes to us as a helpless baby, a troublesome person, as vulnerable flesh, as flesh crucified, as flesh raised – but still, recognisably, flesh. In this way, only God can establish God, not our limited reason and not some malignant fantasy about an infallible book, church or earthly authority.

Rather, it is in the vulnerable, historical, tortured and dying shape of Jesus that God, if we will allow it, melts our hearts of stone and gives us instead hearts of flesh (as Rowan Williams beautifully puts it). On this basis the gift

101

of the risen life, also promised in Jesus, becomes possible. To be saved by God in Christ we have to become more, not less, human, says God, because it is humanity and creation – not laws and theories – that God loves.

Meanwhile we are free, but everywhere in chains, as Rousseau observed and Marx reiterated. But the answer is not a messianic class rising up to bloody their enemies and replace one dictatorship with another. It is, instead, the kind of 'rule' that emanates from One nailed to a tree. What is 'crowned in glory' in the New Testament is not human might and power, but divine weakness, foolishness, the humility of love overcoming the apparent strength of force; the 'yes' embracing the 'no'; the 'nothing' overcoming the supposed 'something'. (The cry of a celebrity culture is, 'I want to be something'; the cry from the gallows is, para-doxically, 'Why have you forsaken me?')

The language I am using here is in one sense 'modern'. But if you read the New Testament you will also see that it is thoroughly biblical. In the offence of the cross, God in Jesus takes everything that the world of power, death, domination, abandonment and torture has to wreak, and endures. It is this that makes a new creation, and new people to fill it, possible. The argument within the Christian community then becomes 'who?' and 'how?' Out of these questions all our age-old theological arguments develop, with some Christians claiming that God's love must win out – though by persuasion, not force – and others retreating into old religious habits that try to divide the world into the insiders and the outsiders (given that the people who see it like this always figure themselves, strangely enough, as 'insiders'!).

These arguments rage in the pages of the New Testament. We cannot settle them from its pages alone. The end of the argument is God, not us. But what is not in doubt is that it is Jesus, and him crucified and risen, that tells us exactly what and who God is. In Christ, everything we thought we knew about God, the world and ourselves turns out to be not the case, and sometimes nothing like the case. This is a result of what theologian John Milbank calls 'the Word made strange'. Now this begs a whole mass of questions, many of which there will not be room for in this chapter, or even in this book, but it does strike me as at least the beginning of something that could genuinely be called Gospel, good news.

So far so good. But . . things aren't quite that easy, for me, for you, for anyone. Admittedly, my problem is not that of an ancient philosopher who needs the world to be 'perfect', and therefore cannot make any sense of this crazy 'god' who gets killed in and as a Palestinian–Jewish peasant of dubious lineage on the margins of empire. That, he (certainly he) reasons, gets you nowhere – except, possibly, the denigration of true learning, and needless encouragement to a bunch of social misfits who cannot see the benefits of civilisation and empire. The first Christians, in other words.

I don't see the world like 'the Greek', but I can name the possible modern equivalents of this mindset: not just the empire builders of all kinds (including me, sometimes), but also the self-proclaimed rationalists who dream of only one kind of reason. They fit God into their categories and then proclaim this 'god' dead and useless. And as for the change of perspective required to see God through the lens of the Crucified One, well that is a step way too far in the opposite direction, an 'anthropomorphic' rendition, they say, little realising that even the most abstract equation is anthropomorphic because dreamt by a human being. The unreason of self-regarding reason knows no bounds.

Then again, my difficulty with 'Christ crucified' isn't that of the pious religious believer formed by the Law, and not just because I struggle with religion, piety and legal systems! To this person, Paul would say, Christ is unnecessary, and, worse, an encumbrance, because there is a perfectly adequate system of religious weights and measures to determine who gets God's favour and who doesn't. What's more, the pious, religious person either knows the system (and can work it to his, less likely her, advantage) or helps to run it. Which does, indeed, help, if you are looking for it to benefit you.

But, instead, what God offers, according to these barmy Christians, is a man who defies the Law (blessing the unclean and healing them, working on the Sabbath, uplifting the poor, profaning holy bread, saying the Temple will collapse – that sort of thing), and is then put to death by the enemies of our people (the Romans) in a way that brings shame and dishonour on us. As for the resurrection, well, some of us expect that, but not for heretics, and not on the hooky say-so of a bunch of women followers whose word cannot even be accepted in a recognised law court.

Put this way, it is not too hard to see the problem both 'Greeks' and 'Jews' (to use the convenient labels of the time)[3] had with the message of Christ crucified. For the Jewish people it still is a big problem, not least because of the calumny, false witness, torture, death and holocaust meted out on them, often in the name of (and with the sanction of) people who claim to be followers of the Crucified. For many Muslims, too, the idea that God could consort to be involved in the dirty, earthly life of Jesus and his shameful death is nothing less than blasphemy. It offends against any reasonable idea, whether 'rational' or 'religious', of who and what God is.

Now as it happens, none of these objections is a problem for me. I hope this is because, as Paul puts it, I am 'being saved'. But, in reality, *that* is part of my problem. I don't want to be saved – not if it involves a radical de-egoising of my life. OK to play at on Sunday, maybe, but I know that isn't what's at stake. There are still plenty of areas of my life in which the scrutiny of the Crucified and Risen Jesus is just too uncomfortable to be felt. Besides, being modern, I am inclined to view the notion that I need 'rescuing' or 'saving' somewhat demeaning, since I don't like to face the fact that if I'm going to live well and in harmony with other people, the earth and God, I need some resources which are a little bit beyond those I can muster myself. And I fear that there might be a 'catch' in getting those resources, because I have been brought up to think of God as a bit like a boss trying to catch you out or subject you to an elaborate regime of rewards and punishments.

Now of course there's plenty in the Bible that can be construed in this way. But only if one does not take as central the life, death and resurrection of Jesus, which, as we keep noting, speaks of God in an altogether different and more (demandingly) gracious way. I know that. But the burden of hearing the Gospel, and knowing that it is about a freedom which only comes by giving up a certain false but consoling view of what constitutes our human autonomy, is a pretty tough 'comfort'. In many ways it would make my life easier to embrace hedonism on the edge of daring despair (I'm wealthy enough for that) or some self-improving 'spirituality' that demands nothing ethical but gives me a warm glow and better prospects of being liked by wealthy, attractive, rich, secure people.

So my situation is not that the cross makes no sense or is an *obvious* offence, but that it makes the wrong kind of sense and the wrong kind of offence. It does not leave me (us) comfortable and unchanged. And, what is more, it still leaves me with a God who apparently identifies with hideous, unbearable torture and death rather than *doing something* about it. This is because the God of Jesus is not a convenience, but a lover. As the playwright Dennis Potter almost put it, when reflecting on his impending death from cancer, God is 'not the bandage, but the wound'.

The 'sense' to be made of this is that God has gifted a universe shot through with freedom. As physicist and theologian John Polkinghorne once put it, 'God has made the world in such a way that it makes itself.' On the plus side, that means we really are free. We have God-given potential. As humans we are constituted, but not finally strangled, by evolution, heredity, upbringing and learning. We can grow to love and be loved, the most glorious thing in the world. But the bad news is that we also have the capacity for almost endless destruction, and that the world is a contingent place in which 'acts of nature' can and do thwart and kill us. And being told that, somehow, God in Christ identifies with our pain and confronts our wrong so as to offer us wholeness which can be tasted but not fully grasped 'here and now'; this isn't the kind of 'solution' that most of us wish for.

Meanwhile, what we are continually faced with is this appalling image of the man dying on the wooden frame, the one that offended Albert. (No, I haven't forgotten him.) What a crucifix says to many is not that God's love is great, expansive, all-embracing and unfathomably powerful in its capacity to endure and transform (as the Gospel would have us believe). No, what it says is that God is a

105

weakling, a sadist, a cosmic underachiever, a failure, a fraud, a fiction and (or) a savage. And if we cannot see this as the other, equally plausible (in purely human terms) construal of what is involved in the crucifixion, then I suspect we are not good at facing facts, and therefore cannot be fully grasped by the wonder and glory of which it speaks either.

Albert had some intuition about this dark side of the cross and of God, and therefore, I sense, is near the Kingdom of God in which he so militantly disbelieves. Rather like the brigands and robbers who were killed with Jesus, and whom he welcomed into God's love, I was going to say. But Albert is a decent bloke, with no criminal or terrorist record to my knowledge, so that seems a bit unfair. But you get the idea. He is also against torture and murder. He refuses as a matter of principle to crucify people. He is against scapegoating, human sacrifice and child abuse.[4] That I know.

Unfortunately, it isn't immediately apparent that all those who most loudly preach 'Christ, and him crucified' are quite in this place. Many wear the badge with pride, but they aren't safe to be with, because they think that forswearing the possibility of killing is 'unrealistic'. I'm pretty sure they're 'okay', but I hope I'm not around when they decide that murdering a fellow member of the Body of Christ might be alright because their country has declared war on me, or whatever. (And no, I'm not saying it's fine to kill anyone else, either. Just spelling out the awful commitment that might actually be involved in baptism.)

Then again, the terrible truth of Christian history (so ably summarised by Giles Fraser in this book) is that the followers of the Lamb who was slain have been only too willing, all too often, to slaughter other lambs. Often for God as well as king, and perhaps as part of some righteous war on an 'evil empire', sanctioned by a superficial (but not entirely inaccurate) reading of the biblical pogroms. Sometimes they have even done this, to fellow believers as well as to non-believers, in the name of Jesus. Now this really *is* hideous blasphemy. But it is not what usually counts as such in contemporary Christian culture.

If you really want to offend Christians in the West today,

don't worry about launching a war, killing thousands, tor-turing, and abusing people in the name of freedom. All but a tiny minority will have no problem with that. No, what you should do is put on *Jerry Springer: The Opera*. This obscure alternative piece of musical theatre, which bril-liantly satirises the amoral and degrading world of 'reality' TV, was a surprise hit in the West End of London. Then it went on BBC television. A very small audience watched it. But, before they had even seen it, tens of thousands of militant Christians protested, cursed and boycotted the broadcast. Why? Because it had a lot of swearing in it, depicted the seamy side of life, and ended up with Springer in hell (the right place for him, according to many Christians, you'd have thought!) hosting an imagined 'greatest ever' production of his TV programme. This fea-tured biblical characters (including God, the Devil, Jesus, Mary, Adam and Eve) arguing with each other about whose fault it really was that the world was in a terrible mess. Not perfectly realised, but quite theologically prom-ising, I'd have thought.

The potential was lost on the protestors, however. But what *really* got up people's noses, apparently, was that Jesus was depicted dressed in a nappy, and was accused of being 'a bit gay' – meaning, I suspect, a bit charmingly inef-fective, as well as (perhaps) of uncertain sexual orientation. Now I don't wish to say that this is a wholesome and pleas-ing image. But I would point out that Christians wrap Jesus in a nappy every Christmas, that the gospels are shock-ingly silent about his marital status (a good rabbi would *surely* have been married), and that ending up tortured to death on a cross is a *far* worse fate than humiliation through unfashionable couture.

I'm sorry if I have offended anyone by putting it this way. Let me assure you that my devotion to Christ is clear and strong. But I can only get my point across by being this blunt. And my point is, firstly, that the offence of a satire (which I suspect offended many simply by going right over their heads) is an offence against taste, for some – though not, in this instance, for me. But compared to the awful calumnies which Christians either ignore or collude with every day, it really rates very low.

Why can't we see this? It is surely offensive to those who are *really* humiliated as prisoners ('when did we see you in prison, Lord?') to get all self-righteous about a rude opera watched late at night by a cultured minority. This shows a truly shocking lack of priorities, a large portion of insensitivity (both to what is really going on in the world, and to the importance of satire itself), and a notable degree of confusion about how Jesus himself dealt with humiliation. He endured it, and remained silent in the face of those who showed no sign of being prepared to hear anything he might have said.

Jesus did not do this, at his trial, in order to model abject passivity, however – another distortion which has been used by wrongheaded Christians to get the poor to accept their degraded lot. He did it as a way of exposing the truth by refusing to be caught in a tissue of lies and death dealing. As Deny Turner once put it: confronted with a cruel but fickle Pilate, Jesus simply refused to converse with a frivolous moraliser – with a ruler who could dissect minor offences while unthinkingly contemplating major calumny. It is striking how many of Jesus' followers do not see it this way. Their (our) instinct is to judge, to cast the first stone, to pay back wrong with wrong (rather than good), to hate our enemies, to curse those who offend us. All anti-Gospel actions.

In other words, when the chips are down, we Christians often have absolutely no idea what the Gospel is about. Unlike Albert, who understood that if he was to take it with due seriousness it was better to protest it than to play at it, and who also saw just how extraordinarily *offensive* everyday Christian speech and imagery about the crucifixion is. So being a sensitive person he understandably wished to veil or do away with the offence. Perfectly reasonable. How shocking that his Christian interlocutors (including me at the time) did not have the moral wit to begin to understand why.

The image and message of Christ *has* to be offensive, however, because it *is* offensive. The killing of an innocent cries out for blood. But Jesus, equally shockingly, will not strike back, disarms Peter and says that among his followers 'it shall not be so'. Where is the ethics in that, colluding with injustice? What is going on here, says St Paul later, is that the powers-that-be are being paraded and mocked by God's corruption-free, violence-free love. This is how the cross makes peace and breaks down barriers. It does so not through some elaborate theological schema; it does it through mockery and derision.

The cross, borne by God in Christ, turns out to be God's shocking, real, political satire of the death-dealing ways we are immersed in as both secular and religious people. To preach 'Christ crucified' is an absolute scandal, but it is a scandal with a point and a possibility of hope that is otherwise entirely missing from conventional political satire. Chris Morris (originator of a controversial mock-documentary traducing media sensationalism in the treatment of paedophilia), eat your heart out. *Jerry Springer: The Opera*, eat your heart out. The cross, the torture and death of a single human (and, by unspeakably foul extension, six million, and more) embodies the ultimate confrontation of evil beyond which no satire is needed.

Yet it is precisely this tree that God makes holy, in which God makes a dwelling place, so that even the place of sin, shame and death cannot be beyond redemption – because the One who offers unconstrained, uncontrollable, unsellable, unbargainable love (that is, the real thing) is there. How? Exactly, we cannot know or say. It is the poetry of real terror, pity and hope, written in actual blood. But if our hearts of stone can be broken by this offence, this stumbling block, then perhaps the way of salvation is indeed possible for us. Beyond paltry reason, yes, but also beyond paltry 'belief'.

'Is anything sacred?' asked those who protested Jesus' honour outside the BBC. The answer is obvious. After this death on the cross, which embraces all death and all degradation, no, nothing is sacred. Did we need to be told? Have we not seen with our own eyes? And yet because of this same event (in some extraordinary way beyond the power of telling), *everything* can be sacred, but only if God is who God is in Christ, reconciling the world; if God is indeed the One who raises the dead to a life beyond corruption, but in continuity with the presence, power and purpose that is at work in the fleshly Jesus.

109

So the truth of the cross is that the salvation God offers is mortgaged on what, in human estimation, is demeaning death. It is this of which Paul speaks so bluntly. It is a sacrifice whose purpose is not to shore up the sacrificial system (as so many Christians want, with their retributive 'satisfaction' ideas), but to demolish it, according to the Letter to the Hebrews. And how do we receive this salvation? By being baptised, which St Paul describes as being taken down into the waters of death with Jesus, in the promise that we will share the risen life God gives. Not exactly what the 'christening party' had in mind last weekend, eh? They thought it was a harmless naming ceremony, not a willingly accepted death sentence. If people really understood baptism, they'd lock us Christians away in an asylum.

And that is my point. To appreciate the cross is to see, without flinching, the sheer offensiveness of who God is in and as Jesus. But we Christians miss the offence (and therefore the true weight of glory) because we have domesticated the cross. In reality the crucifix that Albert objected to wasn't offensive because it really *was* an instrument of torture. It was offensive because it was kitsch, tacky. But that's what we want – not the real thing (which is more like *Jerry Springer: The Opera* than most of what goes on in church), but a fake. A cross with a convenient handle, as the Japanese theologian Kosuke Koyama once tellingly put it.

'We preach Christ crucified.' Imagine, for a moment, if we were shown it as it really is, so that we could see it anew. How would it look? 'We preach Christ beheaded,' perhaps. Or 'We preach Christ in the electric chair.' He had no capital, so let him take the punishment. And what is truly appalling, is that the biblical God is in this – *but as absolute abandonment*. Thus Jesus' cry of utter desolation. God is there by *not* 'being there' as we usually understand it. This is the true atheism. Once we have embraced it, and once the God who is utterly void on the cross embraces us, we will never again be able to 'believe' in anything, and especially not in the powers-that-be whose work is crucifixion. Emptied of religion and belief in a way that self-contrived 'atheism' can never achieve, because that is about *our* strength, we can learn how to resist false gods, knowing the uplifting love of the true God who is beyond our capacity to think, imagine, own or kill. And to whom our only response can be adoration.

## Notes

1 Resurrection is popularly (but wrongly) understood to mean the resuscitation of a corpse. In the parlance of popular culture it is close to reincarnation. St Paul, whose thought about its meaning is the most elaborate in the New Testament, would have had no truck with such fantasy. In saying 'God raised Jesus' he was claiming that Christ had become the first fruits of a 'new creation' in which the power, presence, personality and purpose which was Jesus of Nazareth had been restored to bodily union with God beyond corruption. By 'bodily' he did not mean 'physical' in the usual sense we use it, but incorporation into the transcendent life of God such that the features of an embodied existence are made real in a way that wholly surpasses our present perception of them. He used the paradoxical term 'spiritual body' to denote this, and to distinguish resurrection either from Gnostic immortality myths or from crude physicalist speculations. What is being spoken of is beyond the realms of physics and metaphysics and can be received only by metaphor, not by measurement.
2 I have forsworn the provision of biblical references in this chapter, since readers will learn more by searching for them than being told they are there. Forgive this little didacticism.
3 These labels make me slightly nervous, but only because we live in a time of anti-foreigner and anti-Jewish resurgence again, which makes them liable to fatal misconstrual.
4 Contrast this with Steve Chalke's claim in this book (a correct one, I believe) that the doctrine of 'penal substitution' as believed by many Christians is, unfortunately, a theory that amounts to 'cosmic child abuse'. This is why it is so mistaken and so subversive of true Christian understanding.

# 11 Finding light in the shadow of the cross

### David Wood

The basilica of San Lorenzo in the heart of Florence is on every tourist's list. Consecrated in the year 393 by St Ambrose of Milan, most of us go to see the famous four-teenth-century makeover by Filippo Brunelleschi, and master-works of Donatello and Michaelangelo. Expectation turns to surprise, however, as you walk toward the sanctuary. Over a side altar is the painting *St Joseph and the Christ Child*, dated 1964, by Pietro Annigoni. In this perfectly ordered and harmonious Renaissance interior, set in the calm of Brunelleschi's grey and white architecture, this modern work arrests the eye. The child Jesus stands at the carpenter's bench, guided and protected by his father. Wooden lathes in the foreground direct the gaze upward, evoking the wood of the cross.

But this is not a painting where the *shadow* of the cross falls across the early life of Jesus of Nazareth. In this work, the *light* of the cross hovers over carpenter and apprentice, making sense in advance of all that is yet to be. 'The Lamb was slain before the foundation of the world, and from the beginning the universe was held in existence by the death of the Redeemer. So, had Jesus of Nazareth come down from the cross, creation would have been instantly unmade and time itself unborn.'[1]

This is the Christian view of reality, our characteristic contribution to the human search for meaning, our distinctive way of reading the facts of existence faithfully. The universe, we believe, is made in such a way that giving and self-giving lie at its heart. Ruthlessness is not, after all, the final word. It is not the Word that was made flesh at Bethlehem. 'That birth, and the life and death and resurrection which followed, provide the clue by which we can detect this other law at work in the processes of the universe, one which lies at a deeper level than the stimulus to rivalry and self-preservation. It is the law of self-oblation.'[2]

In other words, the cross, as the climax of a life of sacrificial love, is the indispensable clue to unlock all the mysteries. Real life involves being with God where God is – in the thick of things, in all the passion and pain and tender joy. What we see at Calvary is not defeat, but triumph. Here, at the foot of the cross, we come face to face with the light that shines unquenched by darkness (John 1:5). The great cry of victory rings through the cosmos: 'It is accomplished!' (John 19:30). Jesus crucified achieves God's whole mission. 'All you gave me to do, Father, I have done. I held nothing back for myself. I have emptied myself of ego, given absolutely everything without reserve – myself, my life, my all, a ransom for many.'[3] The tree of shame turns out to be the tree of life, fruiting abundantly.

This is not a case of 'no cross, no glory', for the cross *is* the glory. The date of love's triumph is Good Friday, not Easter Day. On Easter morning, the sun simply rises as usual, the sun which has already vanquished night.[4] The resurrection 'indicates' the cross, setting the divine seal on what is done there. Just as I am pleasantly surprised by the introduction of Pietro Annigoni's vision into San Lorenzo, however, many seem surprised to discover this to be the true meaning of Christ's cross. The default position is an easy sentimentality, some sort of morbid fascination with the dead Jesus and the emotional charge induced by focusing on the extent of his sufferings. Down this murky psychological road lies pietistic individualism and, ultimately, even greater self-centredness and selfishness. Domestication of the cross and the resulting privatised religion at best distorts Calvary, and at worst totally betrays Christ's victory there.

To say this, however, is not for a moment to avoid the grisly truth. Without a doubt crucifixion is a monstrosity, one of the most ingenious forms of torture devised by human cruelty. But the shock of the cross is not how badly Jesus suffered. It is not about imagining Jesus' death

as more terrible than any other. What about those who
lingered on the cross for days? What about the other ways
in which the Roman Empire tortured its non-citizens to
death? What, indeed, about the ways people die still – at
the hands of the state, in police cells the world over, innocent victims of hate crimes or terrorism? Did Jesus really
die a more terrible death than Matthew Shepard?[5] 'We
need, in thinking about the cross, to move beyond the
attempt to bring emotions to the boil by pretending that
this was, by definition, a uniquely awful form of physical
pain.'[6]

Our devotion to the cross is not a way of tearing ourselves apart, and not about pitying Jesus. It is worth
remembering that the only prohibition in the Passion story
is found on the lips of Jesus himself: 'Do not weep for me'
(Luke 23:28). Tears are too shallow. Surface emotions focus
attention on the wrong things. The demand of the cross is
so stark, so matter of fact, so persistent that it can only be
satisfied by a complete change of direction in the quiet
depths of the will.[7] On Good Friday, then, we celebrate the
greatness of God's undefeated, undying, deathless love in
the most paradoxical action any religion knows.[8] Indeed, a
moment's reflection shows that defining the cross princi-
pally in terms of physical torture misses the point. We are
not, after all, concerned with some special intensity of
agony or some abstract transaction to placate God's justice.

Supposedly if Jesus had been pushed over a cliff – as
might have happened at Nazareth – or been made to drink
hemlock in a Roman prison, we should not have found
ourselves singing:

> See from his head, his hands, his feet,
> Sorrow and love flow mingled down,
> Did e'er such love and sorrow meet
> Or thorns compose so rich a crown?

Yet, since the virtue lay in the will to suffer forgivingly,
those other deaths would equally have redeemed
mankind. God's mercy, however, allowed us the poetry as
well. 'How eloquent that physical embrace, "that one
known human signature", that "line athwart another line"
which is the human sign of the Cross. How large that token

of the vulnerable, the open breast, the open palm. The crucified may not clench a defiant fist.'[9] Had we heeded this truth, perhaps Christian history might be less blood-stained.

It is no accident that believers in brutal theories of the atonement tend themselves to be violent in their attitudes and behaviour.[10] After all, we quite naturally reflect the god in whom we believe, fashioning ourselves in the image and likeness of idol or truth. The monster god who demands rough justice in the form of his son's punishment for our sin inevitably produces more monsters. But if we take God's self-disclosure as definitive, rather than continuing our project of inventing god according to limited human imagination, perhaps Christ might be able to speak a word in season to our contemporaries. Our need of the sort of evangelical Catholicism which takes revelation with full seriousness has never been more urgent or necessary. Three cameos may help to earth this reality.

A six-year-old child requires a liver transplant to save his life. As the family waits for a compatible donor, they face the moral dilemma that this gift requires the death of some young healthy adult. After long and anxious months, as their child deteriorates before their eyes, just such a liver becomes available. Delicate surgery successfully follows, the child is making a good recovery, and the parents' anxiety finally begins to fade. Suddenly, for no apparent reason the new liver fails. There is a blockage in one of the major arteries, and nothing can be done. Another transplant is the only hope, at which point the father offers to be a living donor – an exceptionally risky procedure, possibly resulting in his own death. He must weigh his love and commitment to his sick son with his love and responsibility for his wife and second child. In any case, the awful decision is taken out of his hands when it turns out he is not a compatible match. Now it is simply a question of time. Will another liver be available while Ben is still well enough to remain on the transplant list?

As we have all along, the parish community and many friends pray with passion for Ben's life. As his parish priest, I am inevitably living this trauma and walking with his family their way of suffering. By some miracle, or series of miraculous coincidences, a new liver is found before Ben suffers brain damage, he is operated on a second time, and everything turns out well. Five years on, Ben is a healthy eleven-year-old, bursting with life and energy, facing a bright future. We remember too the children he befriended in hospital, the ones who didn't make it.

Is there a God, who is this God, and where is this God in all this? All thoughtful people ask such questions as we live through trauma; they are as natural as breathing. At certain times in human history, everyone seems to be asking them simultaneously. Is there a God, who is this God, and where is this God in the massive disaster unfolding around the Indian Ocean at the beginning of 2005? What are we to say about the millions dead and injured? Is there any meaning in such devastation? Can we possibly hold back the pain, making sense out of nonsense perhaps with a little theology?

The easy certainties of some religious leaders in this moment of truth sound more than hollow; they are blasphemous and morally repugnant. The dean of Saint Andrew's Cathedral in Sydney announces that natural disasters are a divine warning that judgement is imminent. Evidently, God moved the tectonic plates, creating a tidal wave to destroy millions, and chose to do so the day after Christmas. The chief executive of the Australian Federation of Islamic Councils agrees: 'He is testing us – he wants to see how we react to this.'[11] But is God really as capricious, crude and cruel as God's spokesmen believe? And if God really is the celestial puppet-master, pulling all the strings, intent on teaching wayward children harsh lessons, why is God's targeting so casual and God's aim so bad, why so much collateral damage?

One thing becomes crystal clear: the god represented by such officials is not the God of cradle and cross. At Bethlehem and Calvary we see another reality and another power, and this vision relativises everything else we think we know of God, even when we can quote Scripture chapter and verse. The wood of the manger and the wood of the cross open our eyes to a 'christocentric' or 'christocratic' world, infused with and shaped by the divine nature. A different world, where God is always intervening, suspending the

116

laws of nature to protect or to punish would look very different to the world we know. God is not a potentate ordering this or that to happen.

The world is full of chance and accident and God lets it be so because this is the only sort of world in which freedom, development, responsibility and love can come into being.[12] God creates a particular kind of world because God is a particular kind of God, and because God wants us freely to respond to love. More than this, however, God is no distant spectator. The proper name of God is always Emmanuel (Matthew 1:23), for God is always with us, committed to this kind of world in love and to each and every person in it, sharing fully in all the joys and sorrows of life, bearing the cost and the pain of the whole enterprise, giving grace and fortitude and healing and faith to help us through.[13] In the pierced hands of the crucified, we are all held in God's caring, patient, persuasive, passionate, suffering love.

Just in case we somehow miss this in the birth, life, teaching and ministry of Jesus of Nazareth, or if we are inclined to slot such divine revelation into our own pre-existing theological framework, the cross continually confronts us.[14] 'On the cross we see the ultimate reversal of the old idea of providence. The anguished, all too natural prayer was offered, "If it be possible . . ." and it was not possible. There was no intervention, only the terrible silence and a gazing into darkness. And on either side of that silence there was pain – the human suffering and the divine as God and Jesus held firm to the intention that had been there before the foundation of the world: Love bent on creating the possibility of an answering love. So we do not see God averting evil to protect his human child; we see him absorbing evil, letting it come upon him in the person of his human child, and so turning the evil into overwhelming good. That is the essence of forgiveness, the forgiveness of men and women by God and, dare I say it, the forgiveness of God by men and women – God reconciling the world to himself.'[15]

Whether or not we like it, this self-same reconciling God gives us a share in the ministry of reconciliation (2 Corinthians 5:19). In 1999 I found myself betrayed by a

117

friend, a fellow priest I did everything I could to rescue from the consequences of his own misdeeds, who inexplicably turned and devoured me for his own advantage. Living through the shock of evil unleashed, seeing myself and so many others damaged (including, of course, the instigator), witnessing the destruction of years of careful work in just a few months, probably tested my theology more radically than any other experience I have had. Did I still believe any of it? Did any of it make sense? Yet every single time I stood at the eucharistic table in that terribly traumatic year, the truth dawned afresh: in the same night in which he was betrayed Jesus did the best deed of his entire life.

The choice, I realised, was my own. It demanded a complete and conscious change of direction in the quiet depths of the will. I could stand on what little dignity I had left, or take a step too far.[16] Actually, to forgive something you can't forget requires daily *metanoia*, often taking two steps forward and three steps back. At every point, I can store up my resentment or let it go and look to the future. For the cross is no private matter, standing between me and my God, myself as I am and myself as I am redeemed in the imagination of God. It is, of course, always this, but my own redemption is somehow secondary. Essentially, the cross is a cosmic affair, the cosmic love affair between creator and creation. It tells the story of the way things are, of the fire in the equations.[17] It shows us the way the grain of the universe actually runs, inviting us deliberately and consciously to align ourselves with that grain, avoiding the splinters, making the way smooth and straight, a highway for the Lord's royal progress.

The cross shows us how it is possible to absorb evil and neutralise its effects, rather than pass on the anger and live in bitterness. Turning the other cheek, going the extra mile, giving away your coat to the robber who steals your shirt, loving enemies, doing good to those who hate, blessing those who curse us – all this turns out to be an intelligent and intelligible Christian way of living, contributing creatively to the building of cities and the healing of nations (Luke 6:27-38). Here at the cross such costly love is placarded in stark colours, inviting us all to work out our own salvation with fear and trembling and astonishing joy (Philippians 2:12).

## Notes

1 John V. Taylor, *The Go-Between God: The Holy Spirit and the Christian mission* (SCM Classics, 2004), p.180.
2 ibid. p.34.
3 Mark 10:45; Matthew 20:28; Philippians 2:6-11.
4 William Temple, *Readings in St John's Gospel* (Macmillan, 1939), p.357.
5 Beth Loffreda, *Losing Matt Shepard: Life and politics in the aftermath of anti-gay murder* (Columbia University Press, 2000).
6 Rown Williams, 'The Cross in the 21st Century', in E. Newell (ed.), *Seven Words for the Twenty-First Century* (London: DLT, 2002), p.2.
7 John V. Taylor, *Weep Not for Me: Meditations on the cross and resurrection* (WCC, 1986), pp.1-2.
8 Kenneth Stevenson, *Jerusalem Revisited: The liturgical meaning of Holy Week* (The Pastoral Press, 1988), p.54.
9 Kenneth Cragg, *The Christian and Other Religions* (Mowbrays, 1977), pp.112-13.
10 See James Alison, *On Being Liked* (DLT, 2003), pp.17-31.
11. *Sydney Morning Herald*, Tuesday 4 January 2005.
12 Taylor, *Weep Not for Me*, p. 12.
13 Taylor, *Weep Not for Me*, p. 12.
14 See David Wood, *Poet, Priest and Prophet: Bishop John V. Taylor* (CTBI, 2002), pp.184-99.
15 Taylor, *Weep Not for Me*, p. 12.
16 See Robin Green, *A Step Too Far: Explorations into reconciliation* (DLT, 1990).
17 Kitty Ferguson, *The Fire in the Equations: Science, religion and the search for God* (Templeton Press, 2004).

# 12 Resurrection hope and the intelligence of the victim

## James Alison

In the New Testament we are presented with a set of texts that, in different ways, form a common witness to a life and a death, that of Jesus Christ.[1] This is a witness that is structured by the revelatory presence of the resurrection. If there had been no resurrection there would have been no texts, and no guiding understanding of what the life and death of Jesus had been about. Prior to the texts, therefore, is a revelatory experience to a group of people, an event. It is this event that I would like to explore, attempting to find out something of the density of this event as evidenced by the witness that has been put into writing.

In the first place, the resurrection was something that happened to Jesus. It is quite clear from the New Testament accounts that the apostolic group is claiming this. The same Jesus who had been put to death also rose from the dead. His resurrection was as objectively related to him as his death. No one thinks of someone else's death as, in the first place, a subjective experience that happens to the onlooker. Everyone knows that it is something that happens to the person concerned. It is quite plain from the New Testament texts that the resurrection of Jesus was seen as having done something extraordinary and indescribable to that death, which happened to a real person. All the talk of death having been overcome would have been nonsense if the resurrection had not undone the real death undergone by a real person. Any attempt to make out that the death was real enough, but the resurrection was essentially a subjective experience in the lives of the disciples is but an example of modern *eisegesis*, the reading back into the text of our own preferences or assumptions.[2] Now it is quite clear that whatever the apostolic witnesses are describing it was something which broke the categories of easily available speech, something entirely new and unexpected, and furthermore something which they saw as definitive, and unsurpassable. For us to claim that we understand it better than they do is effectively to claim that it was not definitive and unsurpassable, because we, in our understanding have surpassed it and are able to understand it. Considered as an intellectual approach to a text from a different culture it also shows an incapacity for alterity (radical difference), for being able to imagine that something might be being described in the text which in fact blows open all approaches to reality, including our own.

Accepting, then, the apostolic witness to the reality of Jesus' resurrection, we may enquire as to the witnesses' perceptions of that event, and, in particular, to the appearances which were the signs that the event had taken place, and which, as signs, were events in themselves. It would be proper to start by looking at the circumstances of the disciples after the crucifixion and before the resurrection. From their point of view, their relationship with Jesus had suddenly ended. They had all the memories and loose ends of the way Jesus had influenced their lives, but the possibility of reciprocity from Jesus had ended. So, their emotions were held in a vacuum. It was not merely a neutral vacuum, as if they had had nothing to do with Jesus' death; it was a tragic vacuum because of the way they had abandoned and (in Peter's case) denied Jesus. That is to say that along with the beginnings of mourning, there was present the guilt of betrayal, or at least abandonment, of their friend when the going got tough.

The disciples were not only mourning and feeling guilty, but were also severely disappointed. Furthermore, these reactions were held within a generalised fear of what might become of them in the wake of their leader's execution. They were, after all, easily identifiable, probably by both accent and dress, as foreigners, and many were from the region from which Jesus himself had come. As foreigners in the capital of a police state, and ones linked with a major criminal who had just been executed, it is fully understandable that they met behind locked doors.

What we have then, in the apostolic circle, is a group of disillusioned, frightened, guilty, mournful, semi-traitors. It was into their midst exactly as they were that Jesus began to appear, starting on Easter Sunday. The whole Christian understanding of revelation hangs from these appearances: without them there would have been no Christianity.

The first category by which we can approach the density of the witnesses' experience is that of gratuity. The irruption into their midst of Jesus after his death was totally gratuitous. That is to say it was not part of any ordinary human mechanism of reciprocity. Someone who is attacked may attack back, but someone who is killed does not come back to kill. By killing someone we are in fact terminating the possibility of reciprocity on their part. So, the resurrection was completely gratuitous for the disciples: unexpected, it was not part of any human story that any of them knew how to tell (or could know how to tell). It was indeed the beginning of the possibility of a totally new human story.

Nothing in popular Jewish belief in a resurrection on the Last Day had prepared them for this. Furthermore, the resurrection of Jesus was for them something utterly 'other': their first reactions were ones of consternation and difficulty in identifying what was going on. This irruption of what is utterly other is by no means simply a delightful experience. Where the 'customary' other (the people and places who surround one) is often experienced as constraining, this 'customary' other at least gives us a certain sense of security. The 'removed' other, like experiences in foreign lands or in the midst of unforeseen upheavals, is both exciting and frightening – exciting as we see new things and frightening as we appear to be at the mercy of forces we do not know how to control or deal with (how does one cope with an angry foreign policeman whose language one can scarcely understand? Is one not more likely to get a rough deal at his hands than back home?).

The 'utterly' other is then even more exhilarating and terrifying, because it completely throws our frame of reference. It was necessary for the Risen Lord to say 'Why are you troubled?' (Luke 24:38) or, 'Do not be afraid' (Matthew 28:10) or, 'Peace be with you' (John 20:19, 21, 26) when he first appeared, before they were able to glimpse something familiar – and say 'It is the Lord' (John 21:7). Even so, this was not a collapsing of something strange into something familiar after all. The experience seems to have been that the utterly other had a familiar centre without ceasing to be utterly other. That means that it could not be approached as simple *presence* which could so easily be turned into part of what we dominate and control, but was presence always as other – leading the disciples on and out of themselves. So we find the conviction that it is the same Jesus who is present, and present physically, but at the same time a frank recognition that he could not be instantly recognised.

This presence that is utterly other is also physical (as Luke and John attest). In this way the gratuity is emphasised: a ghostly presence could have been part of the 'other' which haunts one – a projection of a guilty conscience (as Herod imagined John the Baptist into rising from the dead, Mark 6:14-16). A physical presence underlines both the continuity of person (the presence of the marks of the crucifixion also attest to this) and the way in which that person is quite outside any scheme of reciprocity, any sort of posthumous vengeance from beyond the grave.

It may seem unnecessary to say so, but this presence is also a *human* presence. It is not as though, after his death, Jesus gave up his pretence of being human, and resurrected as God. Rather, the apostolic witness underlines that he was resurrected as a human being. This is evident from the way in which a clear distinction is made between the Risen Jesus, who is a human being, and at a certain moment ascends to heaven, and the Holy Spirit, which is not a human being.

Part of the nature of the gratuitous presence is that it is also forgiving. The Risen Jesus did not need to say to those who'd run away 'I forgive you': his presence to them was a forgiving presence, was forgiveness as a person. So in Luke and John he gives them power, and commands them, to forgive others, as the way of spreading this presence dynamically in human form. To the disciples themselves the very fact of his gratuitous presence was forgiveness. This enabled their confusion and sorrow to be loosed within them because the focus of their sorrow and guilt and confusion had come back from right outside it, and was not

affected by it. The Risen Jesus was not reciprocating anything done to him, but was a presence of love without
condition.

Now it is worth noting that this gratuitous presence as
forgiveness was only forgiving because there was something to forgive. The forgiveness was not a change of attitude on the part of Jesus or God, but a change in their
relationship to the other of the disciples. If there had been
nothing to forgive, it would still have been possible to perceive the gratuity of the other as simply loving. Because
there was something to forgive, this gratuitous loving is
experienced as forgiveness. Gratuity is experienced as the
lack of retaliation where some sort of retaliation is to be
expected, and then as the giving of something unexpected.
This surprising non-reciprocation is what pulls the person
experiencing it out of the reciprocating mode-of-being, and
enables them to begin to receive and then transmit love as
something simply given.

There is a further dimension which must be brought out
so as less inadequately to describe the presence of the resurrected one to his disciples. This is the way in which Luke
and John both attest that the Risen Jesus still bore the marks
of his death. This insight is difficult to express clearly, but it
means that when Jesus rose, it was not a simple continuation of his life (as if he were simply a few days older), with
his wounds cured by God, but rather that he was given back
to the disciples as simultaneously dead and alive. In the
Risen Lord there is no chronological distance between the
death and the life, rather the complete 'otherness' of the resurrection life is that it is not on the same level as either
human life, or human death, and is thus able to give back
both simultaneously.

The Risen Lord is thus always the crucified-and-risen
Lord. This difficult concept is attested to famously in the
visions of the slaughtered Lamb in Revelation (5:6), where
the triumphant Lamb is triumphant *as* slain, not because
having once been slain, it is now fully recovered. I suspect
that this is what lies behind the difficult Semitic idea that
Jesus was unable to be held by the pangs of death (Acts
2:24): for Jesus merely to have been cured of death, would
mean that the resurrection life was on the same level as

death, merely its contrary, and stronger than it. However, more is shown: the resurrection life has emptied death of its power, by showing the *form* of death (the marks of cruci-fixion) without its content. What is given back is not only the particular act of God in the case of Jesus, of loving him through and beyond the barrier of death, but the permanent way in which God has made of death an empty threat: his gratuitous, loving presence, is always present as overcom-ing death at any given moment. So, the risen presence is of the dead-and-risen one as gratuitous forgiveness revealing love beyond death.

This brings us to a final point about the density of the dynamic of the risen presence to the disciples; one that once mentioned is too obvious to need much illustration. This is the way in which the experience of the Risen Lord was felt to be in some sense definitive, or originary. The Risen Lord was the irruption of something utterly new that was also the beginning of creation, or a new creation. St John's description of the Garden harks back to the Genesis account of creation; Paul talks of a new creation. John and Matthew, in different ways, imply that that final judgement is already realised in the presence of the crucified Lord. The irruption of something originary into history is also the irruption of what is final and definitive. Now this, it seems to me, brings us back to our discussion of an originary scene. For what we have been describing is a revelatory presence that has a quite specific structure: the other as gratuitously forgiving human victim irrupting into the midst of those who were unable to avoid some sort of contamination with complicity in the victimisation.

Here is something quite clear: we have a foundational scene of origin in reverse, in which the victim is uncovered and given back so as to permit a new sort of foundation that does not depend on a cover-up. This permits us to see the resurrection not in the first place as the next step in the chronological continuation of the life of Jesus, as though everybody knew that Jesus prophesied his death and resur-rection, he interpreted his death beforehand in the Last Supper, he died, and then he was resurrected, the next part of the story.

The resurrection is the possibility of a completely new

and previously unimaginable human story, a re-reading of all human stories from a radical perspective that had previously been hidden. It had previously been hidden by the reality of death. So, the resurrection brings the completely new perception of what Jesus' life and death had been about: the Father's interpretation of Jesus' life as hated without cause. By giving him back, the Father permitted a fresh re-reading of the death of Jesus, and of his life and self-interpretation leading up to it, and thus affords a completely new perspective on human victims. Thus, when Paul has his vision on the road to Damascus, he is perceiving exactly the same new regard on human life as previously had been experienced in a public way by the disciples: this is the revelation of God as human victim.

This was the basis of a new understanding, or intelligence, of the life of Jesus that permitted the disciples to go back in their memories and re-interpret what they had witnessed, recalling and making a unified sense out of what had not seemed to possess a unified sense before. The re-reading included, of course, an honest appraisal of their lack of understanding, and indeed of their abandonment and betrayal of their master, and how even *that* was part of what had to happen. The evidence for this is the way they were able to make a unitary sense out of the texts of the Old Testament, pointing to the death of the Messiah.[3] In the appearance of Jesus on the road to Emmaus (Luke 24:25-27) it is exactly this that is indicated:

> 'Oh, how foolish you are, and how slow of heart to believe all that the prophets have declared! Was it not necessary that the Messiah should suffer these things and then enter into his glory?' Then beginning with Moses and all the prophets, he interpreted to them the things about himself in all the Scriptures.

The risen Lord permitted a completely new re-reading not only of his own life and death, but of the way that life and death re-interpreted the Scriptures. It was not that the apostolic group were able to find a whole series of proof texts in the Scriptures to bolster their belief in the Risen Lord, but rather the presence of the crucified-and-risen Lord was suddenly the hermeneutic key permitting a reading of the Hebrew Scriptures that was able to show God's self-revelation as a process leading to a point of culmination of which they were, through no merit of their own, the witnesses.

The apostolic group was perfectly aware that this change was being produced in them in the aftermath of the resurrection, and they give witness to this awareness in their description of the Holy Spirit. In the first place, a clear distinction is made between the presence of the Risen Lord, who is a human being, and the Holy Spirit who is not a human being. This distinction is clearest in Luke/Acts where the Ascension is accomplished before the coming of the Holy Spirit. However, it is implicit in John, where Jesus breathes the Holy Spirit into the disciples on the first evening of Easter.

That is to say, it is not merely the fact that the Risen Lord is present that is the Holy Spirit, but he actually gives them something that is his, but not totally identical with himself. John brings out the difference when he has Jesus tell the disciples that it is to their advantage that he should go, so that another advocate may come (John 16:7), and indicates that the other advocate will bring about an understanding that was not possible before the death of Jesus (John 16:12-13). John also brings out the identity by insisting that it is the things *of Jesus* that the Holy Spirit will bring to mind and reveal (John 16:14-15). This shows that the disciples understood themselves to have received a profound new intelligence into what Jesus had been about, who God is, and who man is, that had not been available before Jesus' death, and became available shortly after his death. This intelligence, which they understood to be the inner dynamic of the whole life and death of Jesus, and what had formed his relationship with his Father, I choose to call the intelligence of the victim.

By this term I do not mean a peculiar sort of intellectual brilliance, some sort of an increase in intelligence quotient. I mean a particular regard on God and humanity made manifest in the life and death of Jesus by his resurrection. So the disciples were able fairly rapidly to re-read the process leading up to Jesus' death as the story of the self-giving and self-revealing victim, who alone had known what was going on. They were able to understand that Jesus' death was not an accidental interruption of a career that was heading in another direction, but rather that his whole life had been lived in a peculiar sort of way *toward* that death, and that he had been aware of this.

It is because of this that all the gospel accounts are focused around the Passion, as the build-up to it. The disciples, then, were aware that the intelligence of the victim that they now possessed was not only a post-resurrection intelligence, but had been a pre-resurrection intelligence in the person of Jesus alone. It was an intelligence that had, all along, been guiding the life and death that they had accompanied and witnessed. What was unique was the way in which, after Jesus' death, they began to be able to tell the story of this life and death not from their own viewpoint, as muddled hangers-on, but from the viewpoint of the dead man, of the one who had become the victim.

It is not as though they had invented a profound new insight into Judaism to honour the memory of a dead teacher. Rather they were now able to see clearly the inner unity of the interpretation of Judaism which their teacher had been explaining to them as with reference to himself. They were able to see his life through his own eyes: that is, tell the story of the lynch from the viewpoint of the victim's own understanding of what was going on, before the lynch, leading up to, and during it.

This intelligence of the victim is not, however, a piece of arcane knowledge passed by a teacher to a group of initiates, a secret to be divulged only to other initiates. Jesus taught perfectly publicly, though the gospels do show that he gave privileged teaching to a few (the twelve), and even among them he was particularly careful in his preparation of Peter, James and John. The difficulty of Jesus' teaching was something to do not in the first place with its own content, but with the constitution of the consciousness of those he was teaching. It was as if they had had a veil over their eyes until after the resurrection. That is to say, what Jesus was revealing was something about which human knowledge is always shrouded in self-deception. The disciples' understanding was (as ours is) formed by what Jesus was trying to change: that is, the constitution of our consciousness in rivalry, and the techniques of survival by exclusion of the other.

What the disciples became aware of after the resurrection was that the person whose consciousness is constituted in rivalry and survival by victimisation does not possess the intelligence of the victim. The beginning of the perception of the intelligence of the victim is already an alteration in what constitutes human consciousness, permitting us to see things from the viewpoint of the victim, and from the point of gratuitous self-donation. This, they saw, was already fully present in Jesus' life: his human awareness was simply not constituted by the same 'other' as their own. It would, of course, take some time to move from the perception that the other who formed and moved Jesus was simply the Father, to the awareness that this meant that the Son was in fact a perfect imitation (or *eikôn*) of the Father, to the awareness that this implied an equality of substance with the Father, and the beginnings of the doctrine of the Trinity.

After the resurrection, the disciples were able to show the way in which what Jesus had been teaching them all along, the intelligence of the victim, was exactly what he had been living, and wanted them to live. Thus Jesus' moral teaching, and his teaching concerning discipleship were able to be understood not as extra features of his life, unrelated to his Passion, but structured by exactly the same intelligence of the victim that led to his Passion. Exactly the same is true of Jesus' understanding of the coming of the Kingdom of God which he preached, which was also the foundation of the new Israel in his victim's death, which he prepared.

So, for instance, the Sermon on the Mount paints a picture of blessedness as being related to the choosing of a life that is not part of the violence and power of the world, going so far as to show solidarity with those who are of no account in this world, even if this means suffering victimisation because of the option taken. The parallel passage to the beatitudes, the parable of the sheep and goats, shows the same intelligence at work: divine judgement is recast entirely in terms of practical human relationship to victims, independent of formal creeds or group belongings. The only relationship that matters in the judgement is that with the victim.

This intelligence is not only present in those passages which obviously and explicitly have to do with victims and persecution (which are not a few), but is present at one remove in all the moral teaching: in the rest of the Sermon on the Mount Jesus gives teaching about the way in which we are constituted in violence – so anger is the equivalent of murder, lust of adultery, and so on. The Law cannot reach this, the constitution of our consciousness (as Paul was to demonstrate forcefully in Galatians and Romans),[4] so Jesus gives a series of teachings about how to break out of violent reciprocity, learning not to be run by the violence of the other (going the second mile and so on). This freedom, when lived, permits us to live gratuitously with relation to others, even if they then victimise us.

Lest this sound too like a strategy for coping with an evil world, or some sort of paranoia, it is important to insist that the disciples' perception, after the resurrection, was that Jesus possessed this intelligence from the beginning, and that the self-giving, the gratuity, was prior to the intelligence. To put this in a different way: Jesus was able to teach about the intelligence of the victim because his human consciousness was not formed in violence but was purely pacifically given and received. Thus he was able to live his life in self-giving, and it was his self-giving that enabled him to understand the intelligence of the victim, and interpret the Jewish Scriptures around this central perception. From the point of view of the disciples, the process was the other way round: as they became possessed of the intelligence of the victim, so they were able to perceive the gratuity which made it possible. But they also perceived that in Jesus, the gratuity was always there, and had made the intelligence of the victim connatural to him: in this world, what a purely gratuitous human presence perceives *is* the intelligence of the victim.

In this way, the evangelists are careful to indicate that there was no 'death wish' in Jesus. It was not as though he wanted to die, and thus become a posthumous martyr and hero. The person who seeks to be martyred in this way is still very much formed by the violent desires of the world: to become a martyr is to engage in a peculiar form of victory over your enemies. John stresses in particular Jesus' freedom with relation to his 'hour', and the way in which he was laying down his life of his own accord (John 10:18): Jesus' self-giving out of freedom was what gave him his intelligence of himself as fulfilling the promises of the Messiah of Israel as victim.

Only the revolution wrought by the intelligence of the victim made this understanding possible. That God is completely without violence, that God is love, was a discovery only made possible by the self-giving of Jesus to death, and therefore the discovery that our awareness of God had, up till then, been distorted by our own complicity in violence, unrecognised and transferred or projected onto God. That distortion is undone. So, the intelligence of the victim works two ways: revealing man, and revealing God, simultaneously.

The intelligence of the victim is simultaneously the definitive demythification of God, and the final undeceiving of humanity. We can only express that simultaneity dialectically, but of course, as a revelation the simultaneity was not dialectical, but gratuitously given: the two discoveries were simultaneous and part of the same discovery. God is entirely purely gratuitous self-giving, and what that looks like in the midst of humanity is like a dead human victim, and what that says about our relationship to God is that we are related to God as to a dead human victim, either in ignorant complicity in the victimisation or, from now on, in the beginnings of a penitent solidarity.

## Notes

1 This is an edited excerpt from James Alison, *The Joy of Being Wrong: Original sin through Easter eyes* (Crossroad, 1998), pp.70-83.
2 I explain and refute the two key forms this denial takes in my book.
3 Including their abandonment of him; see Zechariah 13:7, quoted at Matthew 26:31, Mark 14:27 and John 16:32.
4 See my 'Justification and the Constitution of Consciousness: a new look at Romans and Galatians', in *New Blackfriars* 71 (1990), pp.17-26.

# Notes on the contributors and editors

JAMES ALISON is a Catholic theologian who teaches in Britain and in Latin America. His many books include *Knowing Jesus* (Templegate, 1993) and *The Joy of Being Wrong: Original sin* (Crossroad, 1998).

SIMON BARROW is Co-Director of Ekklesia. He is a theologian, writer and consultant, and was recently General Secretary of the CTBI Churches' Commission on Mission. His next book is *Changing the Subject* (CTBI, 2005).

JONATHAN BARTLEY is the founder and Director of Ekklesia, the theological think tank. He teaches political theology, writes for a range of periodicals, and is author of *The Subversive Manifesto: Lifting the lid on God's politics* (BRF, 2003).

STEVE CHALKE is a Baptist minister at Upton Chapel, London, and founder of Faithworks. His books include *The Lost Message of Jesus* (Zondervan, 2004) with Alan Mann.

GILES FRASER is Vicar of Putney and lecturer in philosophy at Wadham College, Oxford. He is an author and broadcaster for the *Guardian*, the BBC and the *Church Times*. His books include *Redeeming Nietzsche* (Routledge, 2003).

STUART MURRAY is Coordinator of the Anabaptist Network in the UK. Based in Oxford, he is a writer and consultant, working with the church-planting network Urban Expression. His several books include *Post-Christendom* (Paternoster, 2004).

CHED MYERS is a social activist, biblical theologian, and founder of Bartimaeus Cooperative Ministries in Los Angeles, USA. His books include the acclaimed *Binding the Strong Man: A political reading of Mark's story of Jesus* (Orbis, 1989).

MICHAEL NORTHCOTT is Reader in Theology and Christian Ethics at New College, Edinburgh. A Scottish Episcopal Church priest, his books include *An Angel Directs the Storm: Apocalyptic religion and American empire* (I. B. Tauris, 2004).

ANNE RICHARDS is Mission Theology Adviser to the Archbishops' Council, working within the Church of England's Unit on Mission and Public Affairs. She formerly taught English at the University of Oxford. She edited *Presence and Prophecy* (CTBI/CHP, 2002).

KEVIN SCULLY is an Anglican priest. He is Rector of St Matthew's, Bethnal Green. He is also a writer, playwright and actor. His books include *Sensing the Passion* (SPCK, 1997).

VIC THIESSEN is Director of the London Mennonite Centre. His theological interests include peacemaking, social justice and contemporary culture (especially film).

J. DENNY WEAVER is a distinguished Mennonite theologian and Professor of Religion at Bluffton College, Ohio. His books include *The Nonviolent Atonement* (Eerdmans, 2001).

DAVID R. WOOD is Anglican Chaplain to Edith Cowan University and Parish Priest of Grace Church Joondalup, Perth, Western Australia. He is author of *Poet, Priest & Prophet: Bishop John V. Taylor* (CTBI, 2002)

# Select Bibliography

The literature on the atonement and the death of Christ is huge. In this bibliography we have selected titles relevant in various ways to the production of this collection, or cited by individual contributors.

James Alison, *Knowing Jesus* (Templegate, 1993)

James Alison, *The Joy of Being Wrong: Original Sin* (Crossroad, 1998)

Anabaptist Network UK: www.anabaptistnetwork.com

Anselm of Canterbury, *Cur Deus Homo* (Griffin, Farran & Co, 1889)

Gustav Aulén, Christus Victor: *An historical study of the three main types of the idea of the atonement* (Macmillan, 1969)

Simon Barrow, *Changing the Subject: How the Gospel questions our answers* (CTBI, 2005)

Jonathan Bartley, *The Subversive Manifesto: Lifting the lid on God's politics* (Bible Reading Fellowship, 2003)

Marcus J. Borg, *Jesus, A New Vision: Spirit, culture and the life of discipleship* (Harper Collins, 1987)

Rita Nakashima Brock, *Journeys by Heart: A Christology of erotic power* (Crossroad, 1988)

Walter Brueggemann, *The Bible and Postmodern Imagination: Texts under negotiation* (SCM Press, 1993)

James Carroll, *Constantine's Sword: The Church and the Jews: A History* (Houghton Mifflin, 2001)

Steve Chalke with Alan Mann, *The Lost Message of Jesus* (Zondervan, 2004)

James H. Cone, *God of the Oppressed* (SPCK, 1977)

John Driver, *Understanding the Atonement for the Mission of the Church* (Herald Press, 1986)

Cane Hope Felder, *Troubling Biblical Waters* (Orbis, 1989)

Stephen E. Fowl, *Engaging Scripture* (Blackwell, 1998)

Giles Fraser, *Redeeming Nietzsche: The piety of unbelief* (Routledge, 2003)

Alison Futrell, *Blood in the Arena: The spectacle of Roman power* (University of Texas, 1997)

Kathy Galloway, *Walking in Darkness and Light* (St Andrew's Press, 2004)

René Girard (tr. Stephen Bann and Michael Meteer), *Things Hidden Since the Foundation of the World* (Stanford University Press, 1987).

Samuel N. Gordon, '*The Passion of the Christ* as seen through Jewish and Christian Eyes', occasional paper, Chicago Theological Seminary (Winter–Spring 2004)

Carter Heyward, *Saving Jesus From Those Who Are Right: Rethinking what it means to be a Christian* (Fortress Press, 1999)

Julie Hopkins, *Towards a Feminist Christology: Jesus of Nazareth, European and the Christological crisis* (Eerdmans, 1995)

Richard A. Horsley, *Jesus and Empire: The Kingdom of God and the New World Disorder* (Fortress Press, 2003)

Richard A. Horsley and Neil Asher *Silberman, The Message and the Kingdom: How Jesus and Paul ignited a revolution and transformed the Ancient World* (Grosset/Putnam, 1997)

George Eldon Ladd, *A Theology of the New Testament* (Eerdmans, 1974)

Nicholas Lash, *Believing Three Ways in One God* (SCM Press, 1992)

Kenneth Leech, *We Preach Christ Crucified* (Darton, Longman and Todd, 1994)

David Luscombe, *Peter Abelard* (London Historical Association, 1979)

Christopher Marshall, *Beyond Retribution: A New Testament vision for crime, justice and punishment* (Eerdmans, 2001)

John Milbank, *Being Reconciled: Ontology and pardon* (Routledge, 2003)

Marlin E. Miller and Barbara Nelson Gingerich (eds.), *The Church's Peace Witness* (Eerdmans, 1994)

Stuart Murray, *Post-Christendom: Church and mission in a strange new world* (Paternoster, 2004)

Stuart Murray, *Church After Christendom* (Paternoster, 2005)

Ched Myers, *Binding the Strong Man: A political reading of Mark's story of Jesus* (Orbis, 1988)

Michael Northcott, *An Angel Directs the Storm: Apocalyptic religion and the American Empire* (I. B. Taurus, 2004)

Sandra Hack Polaski, *Paul and the Discourse of Power* (Sheffield Academic Press, 1999).

Kevin Scully, *Sensing the Passion* (SPCK, 1997)

R. W. Southern, *Saint Anselm: A portrait in a landscape* (Cambridge University Press, 1999)

Willard M. Swartley (ed.), *Violence Renounced: René Girard, biblical studies and peacemaking* (Pandora Press/Herald Press, 2000)

Thomas Thangaraj, *The Crucified Guru: An experiment in cross-cultural Christology* (Abingdon, 1994)

Martin Thompson, *The Impact of 'The Passion of the Christ' in Churches in England and Wales* (Bible Society, 2004)

Derek Tidball, *The Message of the Cross* (IVP, 2001)

Andre Trocmé, *Jesus and the Nonviolent Revolution* (Herald Press, 1972)

Keith Ward, *What the Bible really teaches: a challenge to fundamentalists* (SPCK, 2004)

J. Denny Weaver, *The Nonviolent Atonement* (Eerdmans, 2001)

Thomas Weidermann, *Emperors and Gladiators* (Routledge, 1992)

Ze'ev Weisman, *Political Satire in the Bible* (Scholar's Press, 1988)

Delores S. Williams, *Sisters in the wilderness: The challenge of womanist God-talk* (Orbis, 1993)

James G. Williams, *The Bible, Violence and the Sacred: Liberation from the myth of sanctioned violence* (Harper Collins, 1991)

Rowan Williams, *On Christian Theology* (Blackwell, 1999)

Walter Wink, *Engaging the Powers: Discernment and resistance in a world of domination* (Fortress Press, 1992) – volume 3 of the 'Powers' trilogy

Nigel Wright, *The Radical Evangelical* (SPCK, 1996)

David Wood, *Poet, Priest and Prophet: Bishop John V. Taylor* (CTBI, 2001)

John Howard Yoder, *The Politics of Jesus: Vicit Agnus Noster* (Eerdmans, 1994)